Freedom Under Siege

The U.S. Constitution After 200 Years

The Ludwig von Mises Institute
Auburn, Alabama
2007

Freedom Under Siege:

The U.S. Constitution After 200 Years

by Ron Paul

The Ludwig von Mises Institute dedicates this book
to all of its generous donors, and in particular:
Mr. and Mrs. Jeremy S. Davis

Dedication

To my children, Ronnie, Lori,
Randy, Robert, Joy and future generations.

TABLE OF CONTENTS

Foreword

Every American who cares about liberty owes a debt to Ron Paul. From his first run for Congress in 1974 through his gallant try for the Senate in 1984 to his present campaign as Presidential candidate of the Libertarian Party, Ron Paul has been an outstanding leader for freedom.

I had the privilege of working as Dr. Paul's chief of staff in Washington. And in the often corrupt and always superficial city of Washington, D.C., he was a beacon of honesty and decency.

Even the advocates of big government came grudgingly to recognize him as the man they couldn't sway, the man they couldn't buy. His only concerns were freedom, peace, the Constitution, and honest money, and these same ideals animate his latest book.

Naturally, the criminals who want your tax dollars in their pockets found Ron Paul hard to deal with. Devotion to principle is not the engine of Capitol Hill. The back-slapping, vote-trading politicians and lobbyists felt uncomfortable around Ron Paul, almost as though their shirt collars were too tight.

Greatness is often lonely, and it is never easy to oppose colleagues or the statist special interests who wanted Ron Paul to act as their errand boy to the Treasury. They were all amazed, and then aghast, at his refusal to play their game.

New Congressmen are always advised, in shady Sam Rayburn's words, "To get along, go along." They're told: "Don't make waves. Vote for the other guy's spending and he'll vote for yours. Do as you're told and you'll be taken care of."

How easy to become part of the system, and reap the rewards of power.

For virtually every Congressman, there is not even a pause before he plunges into the trough. It is, after all, why he entered politics. But that was not why Ron Paul went to Washington. He sought a great rostrum for freedom, and he never sold out. He even opposed public works projects in his own district, a stand that still boggles every politician in America.

As Ron Paul patiently explained, he could hardly criticize federal spending in California while supporting it in Texas. But such consistency was outlandish. No one could believe his ears.

Over the years, Ron Paul's influence grew. Not with the politicians, but with the people. He educated millions, spreading the ideas of Ludwig von Mises and Murray N. Rothbard on runaway government, sound money, and the free market.

Other Congressmen would be flabbergasted to receive thousands of their own constituents' letters telling them to vote like Ron Paul. As Andrew Jackson said, "One man with courage can make a majority."

Ron Paul has helped build the majority for freedom. In his campaigns, in the Congress, with the F.R.E.E. Foundation and the Mises Institute, calmly and without fanfare, he's worked for us and for our children.

How often I saw him at his desk, at 7:00am and at 11:00pm, poring over legislation and committee hearings most other Congressmen ignored, studying Constitutional history and Austrian economics, and writing some of the most eloquent words ever to come out of the Capitol. He worked hard and cheerfully, earning a fraction of his former income as a physician.

He would get angry at the goings-on. And frustrated. But he was never defeated, because he never forgot why he was there. Not to make a career in the State apparatus, but to help dismantle it.

He never made a promise he didn't keep, never violated his oath to uphold the Constitution, never desecrated free market or hard money principles, never voted to waste a cent or to raise our taxes, was never less than a pure champion of liberty.

We have not seen Ron Paul's like in Washington since the days of the Founding Fathers. And this book helps demonstrate why. On the economy, civil liberties, the IRS, foreign policy, the gold standard, the draft, and the Power Elite, he takes the hardcore, principled Libertarian position. He is the 20th century's Thomas Jefferson.

The Omnipotent State threatens us with inflation, expropriation, depression, war, and slavery. Republicans and Democrats offer only lies and loot-seeking.

But Ron Paul and the Libertarian Party provide honesty and decency: an America where we are free to work and to achieve; an America at peace with its citizens and its neighbors; an America of abundance and compassion; an America of healthy families and decent children; an America tolerant of peaceful differences; an America true to its origins in liberty; an America liberated from the Moloch State.

The remaining years of the 20th century hold out the prospect of State-created war, pestilence, famine, oppression, and depravity. If we succeed in changing this specter, Ron Paul and the Libertarian Party will have made the difference.

Llewellyn H. Rockwell, Jr.

Llewellyn H. Rockwell, Jr., is founder and president of the Ludwig von Mises Institute.

Acknowledgements

Special thanks to Lew Rockwell, Carol Paul, Karla Christman, Jean McIver and Nadia Hayes for their assistance in making this book possible.

INTRODUCTION

The People's Manners Are Now Corrupt

Two hundred years ago the United States Constitution was written as a guide for America's unique experiment in freedom. Today the free society that the Founders envisaged is barely identifiable.

America is no longer a bastion of freedom. Prevailing ideology, grounded in economic ignorance and careless disregard for individual liberty, is nurtured by a multitude of self-serving, power-seeking politicians spouting platitudes of compassion for the poor who are created by their own philosophy. Reelection is paramount in the minds of most of those who represent us, while freedom and constitutional restraint of power are considered old-fashioned and unwise.

The feeling of frustration prevalent in the country today is certainly understandable. Government is so big and the bureaucracy so cumbersome that the average person has little to say about his economic destiny unless he resorts to the underground economy. In a free society, of course, individual initiative and ability are the principle factors in determining one's economic well-being.

Not surprisingly, half of the people don't register to vote and less than half of those who do rarely vote. When permitted on the ballot, "None Of The Above" is the most attractive candidate.

Something certainly has gone wrong. The role of government and the people's attitude toward government have changed dramatically since 1787, with most of the changes occurring in the twentieth century. It appears that we are in the waning days of the American Republic.

Has America become known for lies? Our presidents lie about foreign affairs while secretly carrying out activities never approved by Congress. Scientists falsify records for career purposes. Wall Street is filled with stories of lies and scandals. Sadly, lying and deceit have become a way of life for many in America today.

Samuel Adams, at the time of the Constitutional Convention, accurately warned: "Neither the wisest constitution nor the wisest laws will secure the liberty and happiness of a people whose manners are universally corrupt."

We certainly are blessed with a unique and inspired Constitution, probably the best in the history of man, despite its shortcomings. Yet today, two hundred years since its ratification, the Constitution doesn't restrain the pernicious and steady growth of government at the expense of personal liberty. Our manners are now corrupt.

We have been conditioned to accept debt as part of every aspect of our lives. Individuals, corporations, and nations are swimming in debt so great that no one ever expects repayment. The short-term benefit of government borrowing is a political expediency that, in spite of the rhetoric of the balanced budget, is growing ever more popular.

Sadly, we rarely hear serious proposals for limiting the role of government to that of protecting liberty. Both liberals and conservatives give lip service to limited government ideas, but only to serve some special view of government that they might endorse, rather than to promote consistently the principles of freedom.

In the twentieth century we have come to accept demands and needs as rights at the expense of someone else's rights. Responsibility for our own acts and livelihood has been replaced by lawsuits demanding and getting unrealistic settlements.

We have a massive government, passing out wealth stolen from one group and giving it to another. Those with clout in Washington do well, while those who do not understand the lobbying system and seek only their individual freedom are left out. The survival of a car company like Chrysler is now more dependent on lobbying tactics than on management skills.

Government has come to mean something entirely different than what was intended by the writers of the Constitution. It is an entity capable of confiscating and distributing wealth *ad infinitum.* Government no longer serves the people by guaranteeing equal rights to all. Government is now expected to provide profits, medical care, jobs, homes, and food whenever the people demand these benefits as a right. Most people today fail to accept the obvious fact that government largesse can come only as a result of a systematic scheme of government theft.

Compromise is universally accepted as the only tool for political stability, while the leaders argue that anything less is rigid and confrontational and will inevitably lead to chaos. Yet this so-called tool of compromise, on each occasion it is used, is an attack on someone's freedom. Most fail to see that interventionism, welfarism, and socialism are very rigid philosophies. Continued sacrifice of a portion of one's rights has led to a disintegration of self reliance in America today.

The latter part of the twentieth century has permitted the acceptance of the idea that "society" owes everyone a living. Vandalism by many is no longer seen as a crime, but only as an opportunity to get what is deserved or owed to them. Once the principle of government wealth-distribution is accepted at face value, it is logical to expect some individuals to bypass the slow-moving bureaucracy, especially in a time of crisis, and take what they claim is rightfully theirs.

This principle is the reverse of Frederic Bastiat's moral law. Bastiat stated that a law is immoral if it does something that an individual himself is not allowed to do (such as transfer wealth from one to another). Once we accept, as we have these past 75 years, that it's a proper function of government to transfer wealth, it's not difficult to understand the "logic" of the vandal who breaks windows during storms, floods, or power outages and takes whatever he needs without a sense of guilt.

Throughout the twentieth century, the trend has been away from limited government and toward big government's intervening in every aspect of our lives. It has been financed with borrowed money and a fraudulent paper money system.

We have come a long way from the Republic envisioned by the Founders. Today, by majority vote, government can easily cancel out the earnings or rights of individuals without any debate as to constitutionality. The only debate is between the competing special interests, deciding who will benefit and who will suffer. We are witnessing the end stage of the Republic as we drift closer and closer to pure democracy.

Dictatorship of the majority is every bit as oppressive as the dictatorship of the few. It is also more difficult to attack, since so many accept the notion that the majority has the authority to redefine rights.

Political leaders today are more interested in opinion polls than they are in the Constitution and freedom principles. Any event of importance is quickly analyzed by a poll which the politician takes to heart and responds to in an appropriate way.

Keeping up with computer assessments of the people's superficial feelings has been the road to success for many modern politicians. Individuals seeking leadership are prodded to answer incessant and continuous surveys. The leaderless, disorganized, disinterested masses, through poll results, are collectively and unknowingly leading the leaders. These instantaneous recordings, designed to tell the politician what to do, cannot provide reassurance that our rights will be protected in the foreseeable future.

The main problem we face today is that we lack enough champions of freedom. Leadership in the freedom movement has always come from intellectuals who have studied natural law and understood the benefits of the free market. When political oppression is accompanied by serious economic problems, the people will frequently, after years of suffering, overthrow the tyrants. But a wealthy nation, grown soft on the prosperity produced by a previously free generation, tends to vote for that individual who promises the biggest piece of the pie to his constituents. Ironically the prosperity that comes from a free society is the fuel that feeds the fire which brings on the demise of that society. Materially we are much better off today than people were in 1776, but our philosophy of freedom is in much worse shape.

During the twentieth century, America has gone through a transition that has radically changed the political system established by the Founding Fathers. Although many seeds of statism were sown in the nineteenth century, they have matured in the twentieth century.

The trends in legislation in this century are clearly anti-free-market, starting with the Sherman Antitrust Act passed in 1890 to the strong federal control over trade with the Clayton Act of 1914. With the establishment of the FTC to current-day regulations, this century has certainly witnessed a loss of confidence in a truly free market. Even the term "laissez faire" is universally shunned by all politicians who fear that in championing capitalism, support will be lost.

Theodore Roosevelt and Woodrow Wilson revolutionized foreign policy, dramatically changing our traditional belief in neutrality to one of perpetual meddling in the affairs of every nation throughout the world. Today it is mind-boggling that extensive emergency powers are available to the President. Literal dictatorial control of the country is available to an aggressive president faced with a contrived or real crisis. The executive orders, which have the force of law, are issued on a routine basis. Secret agreements and commitments by our presidents are routine and no longer considered unconstitutional. The usual thing is that Congress almost always accepts the secret and dangerous agreements as if they were law.

The year 1913 certainly was a banner year for the anti-constitutional movement. The Sixteenth Amendment, the Personal Income Tax, and the Federal Reserve Act were all passed. The central bank monopoly guaranteed the destruction of our gold dollar. The recessions, depressions, and inflations of the twentieth century can be laid at the doorstep of the Federal Reserve.

Our government routinely lies to us and uses "disinformation."

The Founding Fathers intended that the federal government be totally dependent on the individual states and their legislatures for the collection of taxes and the election of Senators. Since that time, we have abandoned the concept of sovereign individual states and accepted a strong centralized federal government. The Senate was intended to protect states rights and impede the natural tendency of government to grow large, abusive, and centralized. In 1915 the popular election of senators changed our attitudes regarding the protection of the sovereignty of the states. The power of state legislatures to call a constitutional convention, although never used, fortunately is still available to us to circumvent the obstructionist federal Congress. The electoral college emphasized the importance of state power over central authority. This feature, although considered important by the writers of the Constitution, was never a practical part of the election process.

The twentieth century's near deathblow to the concept of individual liberty has today produced a multitude of problems. The people's manners are now universally corrupt. Violent crime continues to grow at a rapid rate and can be expected to continue as economic conditions worsen. One thousand new prisoners are sentenced each week. Many of those who are sentenced should not be, and many of those who are out on the streets, tragically, should be in prison.

Our government routinely lies to us and uses "disinformation." The luxuries of the current generation are financed by the sweat and blood of the next. Yet flowery slogans are used to describe the wonderful prosperity we enjoy, with few realizing the seriousness of the indebtedness incurred in the process. In the midst of a market glut, more and more people each year get pushed into the poverty class.

Liberty has become a term that offends establishment intellectual leaders. Feeble attempts at fairness in the forceful redistribution of wealth is considered noble, but principles that guarantee free-market incentive systems are considered immoral and selfish. Even the businessman today is more accustomed to getting special privileges or contracts from the government than in minimizing the role of government. Difficult choices by our national leaders are postponed, and gimmicks are devised to further consume the wealth and capital of the country instead.

Passion for liberty has faded from the hearts of most Americans and is now cherished only by a remnant diligently working to reestablish its rightful place as one of our most important concerns. The challenge to keep alive the legacy of the Founding Fathers is overwhelming. The Bicentennial Celebration of the Constitution is certainly an appropriate time to restate and emphasize the importance of the freedoms embodied in this great document.

The erosion of freedom seems of little concern where the promise of government security motivates the people and encourages the politicians' extravagant ways. Living for immediate material benefits has replaced concern for long-term freedom principles necessary to guarantee peace and prosperity for the next generation.

American society is characterized by hopelessness and operates without a moral, constitutional, or monetary standard. The early Reagan years permitted a temporary reprieve by glossing over the problems of debt, inflation, and runaway government spending.

A basic understanding of the problems we face is vital if we expect to reestablish the constitutional principle of equal rights:

> Loss of hope in the future has driven many to think only of the present, making a drug-induced high the first priority in many people's lives. Young people feel helpless against their government's inability to provide economic prosperity or safety from a nuclear holocaust. Teenage suicide statistics are a frightening revelation of this feeling of hopelessness.

> The drug craze reflects the desperate feeling of many. Young people remain skeptical of a generation that kills ten times as many with alcohol as with hard drugs and yet pontificates about the dangers

of smoking marijuana. Lack of consistency never contributes to credibility.

Young people cannot help being confused and discouraged if they are fortunate enough to be able to follow the daily newspapers. A 1986 report showed that the federal government ran a 30-year test of radiation exposure experiments on unsuspecting human subjects, making them "nuclear calibration devices."

A lack of understanding of the importance of productivity, savings, and freedom to contract has led to a confused notion of the role of government. Government now operates a $10 billion lottery business, with unrealistic glorification of instant wealth for the lucky (and very rare) winners, while little old ladies who like to play bingo are arrested for breaking anti-gambling laws.

Gambling when done by free citizens without government control is said to be a vicious crime against the state that must be stopped before it destroys the families involved. And yet a government lottery has on numerous occasions in this century been used to decide which 18-year-olds will be placed on the front lines of no-win, undeclared, unconstitutional, immoral wars like Vietnam and Korea. Is it any wonder that young people often are confused and angry and lack long-term goals for the future when their fate can be casually determined by overwhelmingly powerful forces?

Young people, as a result of the welfare ethic accepted today, are not disciplined in the work ethic. Self reliance is not considered important anymore. Somewhere along the way a significant event occurred in our high schools. In the second half of the twentieth century, high school coaches took all the decision-making power from their high school quarterbacks. Although this sounds rather simplistic and irrelevant, it is a reflection of the attitude society has developed regarding the importance of self reliance and responsibility for one's own actions. Today on the high school football fields, only the coaches call the plays. In real life, only the government calls the plays.

America's $10 billion pornographic industry involves the coercive and violent use of children. This industry thrives, while the numbers of hungry and unemployed steadily rise. A nation without standards will see such industries thrive while farmers go bankrupt, oil wells are turned off, and steel mills are closed, and while foreigners outperform us in every industry.

Amazingly, 256,000 millionaires receive Medicare benefits, while the numbers of indigents receiving no care are growing. This is happening in spite of the billions spent with the supposed intention of helping the poor and the down-trodden. The failure of these programs never seems to awaken the people.

Another recent trend reflects a decaying, sick society. Government agencies are bribing citizens to turn in others to law enforcement agencies. Children are encouraged to turn in their parents, employees their employers, and friends their neighbors. Spying for the government is a despicable act and something that should never exist in a free and just society.

There are times when it seems like we get our system of values from television productions. Professional wrestling is one of the few programs which started on TV in the late 1940s and now claims more viewers than ever. There are no rules, and it is associated with contrived (but unreal) violence: mockery of the referee, racism, absence of sportsmanship, yelling, screaming, and hatred. Reasonable rules of decency are totally ignored. The shows get worse every year; belts, chains, and cages are now part of the acts. Twenty wrestlers are put into a ring without a referee and a free-for-all erupts, the more violent, the more the crowd cheers the ridiculous charade.

The twentieth century has been characterized increasingly by guilt. Social planners have conditioned many to believe that problems exist and that we are all responsible. Ideas of collectivism ignore the importance of individual rights and imply social wrongs are "everyone's" fault.

The unbelievable burden of government bureaucracy is enough to depress anyone concerned about freedom.

Madison warned us:

> It will be of little avail to the people that the laws are made by men of their own choice if the laws be so voluminous that they cannot be read or so incoherent that they cannot be understood.

Madison would be apoplectic if he had been forced to witness the writing of the 2,000-page 1986 Tax "Simplification" Act, which no one fully understands. A decade will be required to decipher the thousands of pages of yet-to-be-written regulations. The chaos is not accidental: the taxing authorities can rule any way they wish with those they choose to imprison as long as the tax code is incomprehensible. When our government officials call it "simplification," we can be confident that it is exactly the opposite.

The welfare ethic has destroyed the proper and traditional American role of government's guaranteeing liberty. It has also caused unrealistic and unbelievable litigation that has brought the production of some goods and services to a standstill.

Schools are sued for poor performance of students. Physicians are sued for less than normal children, whether due to nature or the patients' own habits. An accident with a lawn mower used as a hedge trimmer prompted a successful suit against the manufacturer because the injured parties were not warned against such usage. A psychic won a huge award for losing her "powers" following a CAT scan. Doctors have been sued for failing to kill unborn children in abortion procedures that resulted in so-called wrongful lives. Boards of directors of charities are now receiving judgments against them for innocent errors of employees.

To the majority of Americans, the concept of responsibility for one's own actions, has been replaced by the belief that someone else must pay those who demand a handout. The manufacturer of a microwave oven was held liable for damages after a woman's cat died when she placed it in the oven to dry its hair—because there was no warning label on the oven! Can you imagine what Thomas Paine's reaction might have been to such an absurdity?

It is inconceivable that the Constitution was intended to protect life and property in this manner. Today a defect in a product is not required for a successful suit, only the claim that an accident could have been prevented by a specific warning.

Common sense is no longer recognized as something we should expect people to use. Common greed is now the norm in a society that accepts the welfare ethic as a constitutional standard.

The twentieth century has delivered a society totally void of standards. It has created: a chaotic economic system operating on a silly notion about money; a drug craze that involves a large segment of the population, especially the young; a welfare state perpetuated by government theft and considered moral and constitutional, but based on a bizarre concept of rights; and a foreign policy that guarantees perpetual preparation for war and frequently war itself. Without standards of values, a feeling of desperation prevails. We are taught that we cannot know all the answers and that there are no absolutes—and that certainly there are no absolutes regarding rights.

The fatalism that follows leads to the use of drugs, socialist solutions to all our problems, and a cynical use of government power to serve the material benefit of powerful special-interest groups. Inflation has become the norm, debt continues unabated, and terrorism becomes the most frequent tool of the oppressed. The feeling of hopelessness prompts extreme religious movements that offer truth and prosperity. Liberal theologians promote worldwide socialism and even communism in the name of love, human dignity, and rights, while fundamentalists retaliate by offering economic prosperity for those who believe in the literalness of the biblical message and contribute appropriately.

We cannot live forever off the wealth of a previous generation and we cannot enjoy the benefits of liberty if we neither understand nor defend that liberty.

The twentieth century has not been good for world prosperity and peace, something that only comes from a free and moral society. We can no longer assume that we will enjoy the benefits of the traditional American system of government that was embodied in the U.S. Constitution. If a fundamental debate and subsequent restoration of sound constitutional principles do not occur soon, the American way of life cannot continue.

We cannot live forever off the wealth of a previous generation and we cannot enjoy the benefits of liberty if we neither understand nor defend that liberty. If it is true that every generation must earn its freedom, the obligation of this generation is overdue.

Certainly this 200th Anniversary of our Constitution provides an appropriate time to consider the serious discussion of what constitutes a free society and how it can be preserved through constitutional law.

CHAPTER 1

The Concepts of Individual Rights

There is a serious lack of concern for individual rights today. The concept of rights has been distorted to such a degree that the authors of the Constitution would not recognize what is today referred to as a "right." Demands for unearned wealth, based on needs and desires, are now casually accepted as rights. We see little value placed on the traditional concept of equal rights.

This change in the general attitude regarding rights is the most significant event of the twentieth century. It has literally torn us away from the constitutional guidelines given to us by the Founding Fathers two-hundred years ago. The media, the Congress, the courts, and the President reflect the prevailing philosophy of our thought leaders—especially those in our teaching institutions. Without an understanding of the nature of rights, a solution to today's political problems is impossible. The gimmicks won't work, only philosophy works.

People must once again believe that it is in their best interest to support individual rights, just as they now believe it's in their best interest to vote for those who provide food stamps for the poor, corporate bailouts for the rich, and bankers aid for the powerful.

The purpose of government is now dramatically different than that which the eighteenth century writers of the Constitution intended. Government is now broader in scope and bigger in size with a corresponding reduction in individual liberty. A precise definition of individual rights, strictly adhered to, is required to prevent the continued erosion and complete destruction of our once-free society.

The twentieth century has been characterized by the diminishing importance of the individual and the rising importance of the collective.

Prosperity, a wonderful benefit of a free society that we continue to enjoy, has numbed our senses, hindering the motivation required to understand the relationship of individual rights to productive effort. Accumulation of wealth, and its forceful redistribution through government coercion, preoccupies the special interests who determine which politician will represent us in our legislative bodies. Political clout is now more important than economic freedom for achieving financial success.

Rights, as understood by the authors of the Constitution, are not an issue of current debate. Rights today are seen as collective and not something individual. Just as economic theory has become macro and not micro, groups are now thought to have rights rather than individuals. The twentieth century has been characterized by the diminishing importance of the individual and the rising importance of the collective. This lack of definition and confusion regarding rights has caused a hodgepodge of court rulings, bizarre legislation, and needless guilt on the part of many.

Today's Confusion on the Concept of Rights

After two hundred years, the constitutional protection of the right of the individual to life, liberty, and the pursuit of happiness is virtually gone.

Today's current terminology describing rights reflects this sad change. It is commonplace for politicians and those desiring special privileges to refer to: black rights, Hispanic rights, handicap rights, employee rights, student rights, minority rights, women's rights, gay rights, children's rights, Asian-American rights, Jewish rights, AIDS victims' rights, poverty rights, homeless rights, etc.

Until all these terms are dropped and we recognize that only an *individual* has rights, the solution to the mess in which we find ourselves will not be found. The longer we lack a definition of rights, the worse the economic and social problems will become.

Every year new groups organize to demand their "rights." White people who organize and expect the same attention as other groups are quickly and viciously condemned as dangerous bigots. Hispanic, black, and Jewish caucuses can exist in the U.S. Congress, but not a white caucus, demonstrating the absurdity of this approach for achieving rights for everyone.

The welfare ethic now universally accepted at all government levels determines the concept of rights. No longer are rights individual but they are based on demands, needs, and greed.

When Lee Iaccoca came before the House Banking Committee on which I sat, he made the "right" of Chrysler workers to keep their jobs the issue, not government largesse for a failing corporation. He explained in his autobiography that the issue had to be workers' needs or he could not obtain the bailout. Since the concept of rights is currently so inexact, he had no difficulty convincing the Congress. The rights of the small businessman who had his credit "stolen" and was forced into bankruptcy due to the Chrysler bailout was not easily identified and thus ignored.

The individual who dares to demand to be left alone and to assume responsibility for himself becomes a criminal.

Careless disregard for liberty allows politicians to promise anything in order to be reelected. Inevitably this leads to a steady increase in spending, forcing higher taxes, more borrowing, and inflation of the money supply.

Government by majority rule has replaced strict protection of the individual from government abuse. Right of property ownership has been replaced with the forced redistribution of wealth and property, without concern for the individual producing the wealth.

Once the dictatorial power of a majority is accepted as legitimate, the days for the Republic are numbered—which is the case unless current trends are reversed. The individual, throughout this century, has suffered greatly from this dramatic change in attitude. The individual who dares to demand to be left alone and to assume responsibility for himself becomes a criminal. Amish farmers have been arrested for not paying social security taxes, though they sought no aid from the government. Any independence from government welfare programs is deeply frowned upon. Those failing to keep financial records for the IRS are promptly imprisoned.

The good of "society" has replaced the notion that the individual has a sacred right to live unmolested by government interference.

Today it is usual to assume that the government owns all that we produce, and through government generosity we are permitted to retain a certain portion. We routinely hear that if a particular tax is reduced, it will be a "cost" to government. This concept must be changed if the idea of individual liberty is to survive. There is no such thing as cost to government. There is only cost to people. Government cannot grant to us our right to life and liberty, it would mean that government controls all that we produce. Sadly this is essentially the situation in which we find ourselves today.

Government's intrusive role has grown throughout the twentieth century, while individual responsibility has correspondingly diminished. The expansion of government control over our lives is both a result and cause of individuals' assuming less responsibility for themselves. Failure today is rarely blamed on the inadequacy of the individual; society and environment are blamed for all our problems. Criminal acts are frequently excused as being the result of "bad breaks." Justifying welfare on the needs of individuals has been upheld and expanded by the courts.

Careless disregard for individual rights, concern for group demands, and concern for the good of society have led to a steady erosion of privacy. Billions of dollars are spent yearly keeping records for the government.

The people, like lambs, are innocently driven to the slaughter as they conform to all the government regulations and record-keeping—records that frequently are used against them in a court of law.

We all naively and obediently become tax collectors for the government, turning over the loot that the politicians will waste as they further destroy our right to live as we choose.

We keep volumes of financial records solely for the government's benefit. We accept currency controls with barely a whimper. We allow the FBI and CIA to snoop on everything and everybody, and rarely is the snooping challenged on principle. The only challenge to the secrecy of government action is whether the activity is supported by the right or left.

The Computer Age is now upon us, and this technology could easily eliminate completely the privacy that should be cherished by all freedom-loving individuals. Like nuclear power, computer technology can enhance our standard of living or destroy our freedoms completely. It is just a matter of time until we have a mandatory national I.D. card.

Lie-detector tests and urine and blood tests are now common-place and have been strongly supported by the Reagan Administration—an administration that claimed to champion limited government principles. Today the government sends out planes and helicopters to spy on farmlands and industrial plants, taking pictures while looking for information about drugs and violation of EPA regulations—regulations which no one clearly understands.

It is inevitable that, once the concept of absolute individual rights is ignored, with each attempt to solve a problem, two new ones replace it. Malcolm Forbes was asked whether his listing in his magazine of the 400 wealthiest Americans would draw the attention of terrorists. His answer was affirmative: "I think the terror most people are concerned with is the IRS."

Today the lack of understanding and respect for voluntary contracts has totally confused the issue that in a free society an individual can own and control property and run his or her business as he or she chooses. The idea that the social do-gooder can legislate a system which forces industry to pay men and women by comparable worth standards boggles the mind and further destroys our competitiveness in a world economy.

Employee rights are said to be valid when employers pressure employees into sexual activity. Why don't they quit once the so-called harassment starts? Obviously the morals of the harasser cannot be defended, but how can the harassee escape some responsibility for the problem? Seeking protection under civil rights legislation is hardly acceptable. If force was clearly used, that is another story, but pressure and submission is hardly an example of a violation of one's employment rights.

The concept of equal pay for equal work is not only an impossible task, it can only be accomplished with the total rejection of the idea of the voluntary contract. By what right does the government assume power to tell an airline it must hire unattractive women if it does not want to? The idea that a businessman must hire anyone and is prevented from firing anyone for any reason he chooses and in the name of rights is a clear indication that the basic concept of a free society has been lost.

In the name of equal rights, the State of Montana has forced insurance companies to charge women additional premiums to make the fees equal to those charged men, regardless of the economic realities that allow for a lower premium.

Americans today have more people living on the street than ever before, in spite of the hundreds of billions of dollars spent to eradicate poverty. Of course, logic tells us that if you subsidize poverty, you'll get more of it.

New York City is plagued with thousands of street people. On cold nights this tragedy is more apparent. Mayor Koch's approach to protecting the "rights" of the street people is to sue hotels which refuse to house the homeless tramps. Another attempt to solve the problem has been to round up and force the vagrants into shelters—to eliminate the embarrassment of people dying on Wall Street. The American Civil Liberties Union has come to the rescue, saying "arresting" the homeless against their will violates their rights as citizens—a reasonable assumption. But the ACLU provides another solution by claiming the poor have "a right to a decent home." The problem, they state, is the failure of government to provide (or steal) sufficient funds to build enough tenement housing. This confused notion of rights regarding the New York street people demonstrates clearly how poorly the concept of rights is understood today in America.

Much of the confusion over rights comes from the accepted idea that "compromise" is the most noble trait of today's politician—hardly a characteristic of those who signed and defended our Declaration of Independence. It is hardly reassuring that giving in halfway is the most important political act of our twentieth-century politicians. Standing firm on principles is viewed as illogical rigidity and dangerous to America. This idea clearly ignores the fact that philosophy of compromise and acceptance of the philosophy of pragmatism is a rigid philosophy in itself which attacks individual rights. Although many justify interventionism as a compromise between socialism and laissez faire, interventionism is also a precise philosophy and not a compromise at all. It requires a sacrifice of freedom from those who give mere lip service to the Constitution and to the concept of individual rights.

Until it's respectable once again to champion individual rights and very limited government, we cannot expect to reverse the trend in which we as Americans find ourselves. Tokenism won't work. Clearly defining the seriousness of the problem and stating what is required to change our direction is absolutely necessary for the survival of freedom in America.

In the infinite wisdom of our twentieth century, courts and legislative bodies have decided that there are two kinds of speech: commercial and literary. Liberals who envy wealthy businessmen support free speech, but advocate strict control over commercial speech. Conservatives, who defend free commercial speech, carelessly support control over literary speech. Somewhere in the twentieth century, we lost our way with accepting this distinction.

The right of commercial speech and business activity are thought to be something quite different from the right to publish whatever one desires and live a lifestyle of one's choosing. The liberal has refused censorship of any journalistic production, yet has never applied the same principle to the entrepreneur who produces a commercial product rather than a book. It doesn't bother conservatives to write laws regulating printed matter of a sexual nature which they see as offensive and harmful to society. Liberals are unconcerned about their attack on the businessman's freedom of speech by regulating ads for alcohol, cigarettes, and gambling, as well as controlling the manufacture of consumer products.

Rules of fraud and product liability could surely be applied to consumer goods, just as the rules of libel apply to the written or spoken product. This discrepancy in dealing with commercial and literary speech must someday be resolved if liberty is to be defended consistently.

When selected prosecution occurs, it is a clear signal that the concept of equal rights is no longer honored. Today it is commonplace to select special people and make them examples. It's the IRS's public policy to make certain key community citizens examples in order to terrorize the other segment of the population into submitting to the tax authorities. In spite of the fact that even the IRS can't agree on the meaning of the massive tax code and the regulations which are frequently never written, the taxpayer is never excused for filing errors.

In a free society, governments are not permitted to break the law for any reason.

Constitutionalists who understand the corrupt nature of our monetary system are likely targets of an aggressive Justice Department, although the litigants are nonaggressive as they practice civil disobedience in seeking favorable court rulings.

Resisters to draft registration have been too numerous to prosecute.

The vocal opponents, those who publicly express their views that such registration is unconstitutional, have been singled out as particularly dangerous and prosecuted precisely because they spoke out.

In a free society, governments are not permitted to break the law for any reason. Yet it has become common for legal authorities to entice citizens, through entrapment, into breaking the law. Tempting individuals and officials with bribes or solicitation of prostitution or offering drugs is frequently done. FBI sting operations and Abscam-type operations are accepted procedures for the Justice Department, permitting officers *of* the law to *break* the law to get others to do the same.

When *U.S. News* reporter Daniloff received "secret" papers from Soviet KGB agents in Moscow and was arrested, U.S. officials were outraged at the nasty trick and called it a "set-up." Yet this is the identical procedure followed by our government against our own citizens.

The New York Times explains editorially the purpose of zoning (November 24, 1986): "Zoning has helped establish the principle that the interests of property owners must yield to those of the public." Zoning under current law, according to *The New York Times*, is inadequate, and the public demands that more controls are needed to assure a proper working and living environment. The only problem is, "who is the public" and why are ownership rights subservient to public interest? I'm sure *The New York Times* editors have a precise idea of who the public is and how its interest is best served, according to their definition, but clearly it clashes with the entire philosophic concept of private property ownership. If the concept of privately owned property's being used "for the public interest" is not challenged, the ideas of socialism will emerge victorious.

If welfare needs of any segment of society can be granted against the wishes of society's productive segment, private property ownership will disappear. If property can be confiscated by the arbitrary actions of the state, the individual will also be expected to serve the state on command.

The more authoritarian the government is over the economy, the more authoritarian it will be over the use of young people in forcing them to serve in the military or national youth service to achieve what those in power determine is in the "public good." In a free society, the individual cannot be forced into serving the state, and the property he owns cannot be confiscated for any reason, even that of a humanitarian nature. The needs of one person cannot be used to justify the victimization of another by robbing him of the fruits of his labor.

Traditionally the family has been the core unit in America, with parents in charge of their children until adulthood. This means they are responsible for their physical well-being, providing proper care and guidance. Permission, until recently, to treat a child medically was always granted by the parent, and without proper consent, medical personnel were considered in violation of the parents' rights if treatment were rendered. Today, permission (and frequently the financing) for this treatment is given by the state to the medical profession to treat adolescents. It has gotten to the point where the M.D. is absolutely protected and relieved of any responsibility to the parents. Twelve-year-old children deserve respect, love, and treatment in a nonviolent manner, but parents who raise and are responsible for their children deserve to know what others may be doing to them. Don't parents deserve at least the same respect regarding their children as others expect regarding their property?

When the state replaces the role of the parent in giving permission for medical treatment, a serious flaw is introduced which is likely to undermine our free society. Since a child is unable to assume responsibility for himself or herself, the only choices are the parents (or legal guardians) or the government. The government, through court rulings or legislation, should never be permitted to perform the role of the parent.

Assuming responsibility for one's own acts was further undermined by the Texas Supreme Court's 1986 ruling that a bartender was responsible for the accident which one of his customers caused after leaving the establishment. This is a perfect example of what happens when no one knows what individual rights are! Once this concept is lost, the idea of self-responsibility is lost as well.

Since the Great Depression of the 1930's, federal laws have curtailed individuals' rights to work in their own homes. The Founding Fathers, I'm sure, never dreamed this could happen in the United States of America. Union workers prompted this law to prohibit low-cost labor from doing jobs on a piecemeal basis. No wonder the U.S. industry lost out to the low-cost labor markets of Japan, Taiwan, and Korea!

Privacy is one of the most sacred elements of a free society

In 1986, after fifty years, a modification of the law was made. But there was a Computer Age IRS catch. People who wanted to work at home (which many continue to do anyway) could do so if they got a certificate of permission from the Department of Labor. The United States is considered a free country, and yet a permit from the federal government is needed to sew clothes in our own homes. My guess is that this little change was more likely motivated by the desire of the IRS to find out where the activity was, than to take a bold step in the direction of freeing up the labor market.

In America we see excellent private homes for wayward children, more successful than any state-run institution, being closed down by the heavy hand of the government when owners refuse, for religious reasons, to buy state licenses. This is done in the name of protecting the children from harsh treatment. All evidence shows that the religious homes for children are far superior to anything the state has to offer, yet are closed for failure to register with the state. This is more evidence that the state now controls our children, not parents or (non-state-designated) guardians.

Articles appear in medical journals debating whether choosing a physician is a right or a luxury. (It's a shame that the correct answer is not automatically known by everyone!)

The confusion over rights has caused numerous debates, such as whether women have the right to join men's clubs. Women obviously have a right to apply for membership in any group they wish, and a club has a similar right to exclude anyone it wishes.

But the great debate goes on. A woman recently sued the Boy Scouts because she claimed she had a right to be scout master. Women may want to be scout masters, but where did they get this "right" to coerce a private organization to change its rules regarding members and leaders?

Privacy is one of the most sacred elements of a free society. It is now common to pass laws which routinely violate the Constitutional guarantee that our homes and persons are not to be invaded by government agents.

When the title of a law incorporates the word "privacy," in true 1984 "new-speak" fashion, you can be certain it means the opposite. Government secrets are more sacred in today's society than individual privacy. When government information leaks occur, the FBI is called in to "protect" government secrecy. The CIA, with its independent operations and funding, is a law unto itself, engaging in war activities, conspiracy, and assassination. Oliver North, with a straight face, on national television, magnificently defended the "right" of the government to lie about covert activities. The only resistance lying gets is when policy offends either the conservative or liberal wing of the interventionists.

Victims of the disease AIDS argue, with no qualms of inconsistency about rights, for crash research programs (to be paid for by people who don't have AIDS), demanding a cure. And it's done in the name of rights. The victims demand health care as well and scream "discrimination" if insurance companies claim they have a right to refuse to issue a policy to someone already infected with the AIDS virus. The rights of the insurance company owners are not considered, while legislation is passed forcing insurance companies to provide the insurance demanded by the victims. The individual suffering from AIDS certainly is a victim—frequently a victim of his own lifestyle—but this same individual victimizes innocent citizens by forcing them to pay for his care. Crash research programs are hardly something, I believe, the Founding Fathers intended when they talked about equal rights.

The Supreme Court, in 1987, ruled that persons with contagious diseases are "handicapped" and are entitled to protection under affirmative action rules. If a person is fired because he has AIDS, typhoid fever, or hepatitis, he can now pursue his case in court.

Recently an alcoholic who developed cirrhosis of the liver demanded a liver transplant, in the name of "equal rights." The state welfare program assumed the obligation to provide care for the man, but insisted he quit his alcoholic ways. The man refused, and the state held up on his liver transplant. For this reason he sued the state, demanding his rights.

With confusion regarding rights, the end of constitutionally protected liberty cannot be far off.

Society is filled with competing interests demanding their "rights." Since no serious attempt has been made to define rights and limit government's power to masquerade as economic equality in equal rights, the confusion gets worse every year.

This is a serious flaw in today's political philosophy and, unless the nature of the problem is identified, freedom in America cannot survive. A lack of a precise standard for describing individual rights will destroy the American way of life—that gift from the Founding Fathers from which we have all benefited.

Trial by Jury—The Ultimate Protection

According to Lysander Spooner, a mid-nineteenth-century writer, there are five separate tribunals protecting us from abusive government laws: The House of Representatives, the Senate, the Executive, the Courts, and the Common-Law Jury. He maintains that all are important but that the ultimate protection of our liberty must be placed in the hands of our peers. His "Essay on the Trial by Jury" (1852) deserves close study by all twentieth-century students concerned about the future of freedom in America.

The concept of protecting individual rights from the heavy hand of government through the common-law jury is as old as the Magna Carta (1215 A.D.). The Founding Fathers were keenly aware of this principle and incorporated it into our Constitution.

John Jay, the first Chief Justice of the Supreme Court, agreed with this principle. In his first jury trial in 1794 (Georgia vs. Brailsford) he stated: "You had nevertheless a right to take upon yourselves to judge of both, and to determine the law as well as the fact controversy." Jefferson was in agreement as well: "To consider judges as the ultimate arbiters of all constitutional questions is a very dangerous doctrine indeed and one which would place us under the despotism of an oligarchy."

The twentieth century, however, has witnessed a serious erosion of this principle. Since 1895 (Sparf vs. United States), the right of the jury to rule on the justice and constitutionality of the law, as well as the facts in the case, was seriously undermined. Also the lack of concern and understanding for individual rights has affected jurors, just as it has representatives, senators, judges, and presidents. Jurors in recent times have been just as guilty of ignoring the principle of equal rights as have our representatives in our legislatures, judiciary, and executive bodies of government. These two factors have greatly diminished the value of the jury in the twentieth century.

Those frustrated with changes in the Congress, the executive, and the judiciary—and there is certainly good reason for frustration—must consider educating potential jurors as to the importance of the common-law jury and the principles of individual liberty.

An awakened citizenry, participating in juries around the country, could bring about a nonviolent revolution of magnificent proportions, reversing the sad trends of the twentieth century. The jury today is a weak institution, as are all the other institutions designed to guarantee individual liberty. The right effort could revitalize the jury and restore it to its rightful place in curtailing the endless growth of an all-powerful state.

Several legal events need to occur in order for big government to thrive. The de-emphasis of the jury was crucial in the expansive powers of the omnipresent state. Judging the moral intent and the constitutionality of the law is no longer even a consideration of the jury. Today the judge instructs the jury to consider only the facts of the case, and then the judge becomes the sole arbiter of evidence admissible in court. The jury system today has become progressively weak over the past ninety years. In addition, judges write into their rulings grand designs for society. Our judiciary bodies have become legislative bodies.

A major part of the judicial system has been removed from the people by placing it in administrative branches of government. The agencies of government have usurped power unimagined by the authors of the Constitution. Administrative justice is a great bureaucracy, independent of the legal judiciary.

The right effort could revitalize the jury and restore it to its rightful place in curtailing the endless growth of an all-powerful state.

Regulations are written yearly by the thousands of pages, read by few, and understood by no one. This is done intentionally to keep the peasants humble and to harass the people. It is used as a political tool for selective prosecution. Regulations can favor certain industries while destroying others, providing great accumulation of wealth for the beneficiaries.

Exemption from prosecution of some while others are pursued has destroyed many good industries and companies. Prosecution in the administrative courts requires great sums of money for self defense. Juries are not available, and one is considered guilty until proven otherwise. Tragically, economic conditions usually prompt the businessman to pay the fine, regardless of its unfairness, to save legal costs. Fighting the system through political reform is not even a serious consideration. Those who would consider such a struggle are ridiculed as idealistic and unrealistic. A powerful political action committee and a shrewd lobbyist are today considered the best investments. Since we have lived with massive bureaucracy for over fifty years, most citizens, uneducated in the ways of equal rights, justice, and freedom, are unaware of any other system. By writing regulations with the force of law and administrative justice, interpretations, and enforcement of these laws, the judiciary ''rulers'' have made a mockery of Article I, Section 1 of the Constitution.

Whether it's in the regular courts or the administrative courts, judges who grew up under the welfare ethic, rarely concern themselves with the right to own and control the fruits of one's own labor. The "right of society," as they see it, precludes what they claim is a narrow self-interest—the individual.

Spooner argues eloquently for the right of the jury to pass final judgment on all laws, the moral intent of the law, the constitutionality of the law, the facts of the case, and the moral intent of the accused. Spooner's argument for allowing such responsibility to rest with the accused peers is that delegating responsibility only to the representatives in Washington was fraught with danger. He was convinced that all government officials were untrustworthy and susceptible to bribery and that removal of our representatives in the next election was not sufficient to protect the people from unwise and meddling legislation.

If we had heeded the admonitions of Lysander Spooner, we would not be faced with this crisis. Spooner begins his essay on trial by jury by clearly stating the importance of the jury's responsibility to judge the law as well as the facts in the case before them:

> For more than six-hundred years, that is, since the Magna Carta, in 1215, there has been no clearer principle of English or American constitutional law, than that, in criminal cases. It is not only the right and duty of juries to judge what are the facts, what is the law, and what was the moral intent of the accused; but it is also their right and their primary and paramount duty to judge the justice of the law and to hold all laws invalid, that are in their opinion, unjust or oppressive, and all persons guiltless in violating or resisting the execution of such laws.

Spooner was highly critical of the phrase "according to the evidence" in the oath of jurors, claiming it violated the classical common law. He states:

> If the government can dictate the evidence, and require the jury to decide according to that evidence, it necessarily dictates the conclusion to which they must arrive. In that case the trial is really a trial by the government, not by the jury. The jury cannot try an issue unless they determine what evidence shall be admitted. The ancient oath, it will be observed, says nothing about 'according to the evidence.'

If a law is assumed to be correct constitutionally and morally merely because it's a law written by our chosen representative, the government can give itself dictatorial powers. And that's exactly what has happened with the massive powers delegated to the President under the Emergency Powers Act—power sitting there to be grabbed and used at the hint of a crisis.

Spooner saw the jury as the last guard against such usurpation of the people's rights. Sadly, that protection is just about gone. It is up to us to restore the principle of trial by jury to its rightful place of importance.

Right to Own Guns and Gold

Spooner had an interesting explanation about why the Founding Fathers included the Second Amendment in the Constitution. He never once considered that the authors of the Constitution meant that only the militia were allowed to possess weapons, as today's liberals argue. He even considered it foolish to claim private gun ownership was for the purpose of defending one's life and property from robbers and murderers. "That" he states, "is so obvious one need not state it." According to Spooner, the real reason for individual gun ownership was for the purpose of protecting against the evil use of government power—as the revolutionaries experienced at the hands of King George III. In other words, when all else fails, the gun owned by the individual is to be used to protect against the tyranny of the state—something obviously denied the citizens of an oppressive state such as Poland or the Soviet Union.

Even though political conditions have deteriorated throughout the twentieth century, American citizens still retain rights superior to most nations of the world. With concerted political action and an awakened citizenry we still have the vehicle to change conditions—something that may not be available to us for an indefinite period of time.

As long as the individual retains the right to own guns and gold, we should assume that working through the political process is worthwhile. The confiscation of gold and guns in the United States would ignite an explosion of physical resistance which would permanently change the character of the United States.

It will come to this if the majority of our leaders do not soon redefine individual rights, restore a free-market economy, and force our government to live within its means.

Without this new direction, the growing economic and political crisis will worsen and can only be temporarily held together by further expanding the role of government at the expense of liberty.

If we do not have a consensus of what "rights" are, there is little chance our free society will survive.

Government snooping, blood testing, lie-detection tests, restraints on financial freedom, stronger IRS regulations, national I.D. cards, and restrictions on travel will all be used to prop the tottering state if necessary.

A lot is at stake, and we cannot erroneously assume America will survive, regardless of what we as a people do. What we do *will* make a difference. And if we do not have a consensus of what "rights" are, there is little chance our free society will survive.

Legislating Morality or Moral Law

Man, throughout history, has been tempted with power. Someone is always ready and anxious to use force over others, both within and outside of government, for his own interest. Some who reject the use of physical power over others and reject the material benefits of illicit power will, nevertheless, use government force to impose their social standards on others. It's important to recognize that there is a difference between legislating morality and moral law.

The following is a *Freedom Report* essay written in 1982 addressing this subject.

Legislating Morality:

How many times have you heard it said: "Government should not legislate morality?"

When the liberals push laws mandating quota systems, integration of privately owned property, welfare aid, medical care for the poor, foreign aid to third-world nations or minimum wage laws, they do it in the name of morality, claiming the nation as a whole has a moral obligation to fulfill the needs of others.

The conservatives quickly retort: "Government shouldn't be legislating morality," claiming it's impossible to force people to be generous, fair, and tolerant. In attempting to "legislate morality," the economic and social conditions which were to be improved by the legislation usually get worse. For instance, integration by busing caused white flight and growth of private schools, creating more black ghettos today than existed prior to the mandate for the integration nearly thirty years ago.

The attempt, in the name of morality, to wipe out poverty destroys incentives and causes economic conditions to deteriorate. Minimum wage laws lead to unemployment and third-world subsidies turn out to be nothing more than bail-outs for New York banks and foreign dictators.

It's obvious that "legislating morality," as the conservatives claim, is a total failure and should be rejected. The liberal "do-gooders," although well-motivated, create more problems than they solve—all in the name of a moral obligation to care for the less fortunate of society. They don't ask why some are less fortunate than others, and never question whether previous government interference may have been the cause and, therefore, cannot be the solution, no matter how well-motivated the intentions of the do-gooders.

For many decades, the political activism of liberal church groups has reflected this belief in legislating morality. They were, and still are to a large degree, "out-front" on many economic and social issues, requesting and lobbying for social legislation from Medicaid to busing, from foreign aid to food stamps. Promoting these programs in the name of the church and morality carries with it a tone of condescension and righteousness. It attacks the very roots of the conservative conviction that free enterprise and the profit motive are sacred institutions.

The conservatives, angry and frustrated since they lack a consistent defense, respond only with the cliche, "government shouldn't legislate morality." The conservative anger exists because the liberals attack the sacred notion of a competitive free market, and the frustration occurs because deep down inside they know that there indeed is a relationship between morality and the law. It is understanding this relationship which has been elusive, causing consternation in many sincere liberals and conservatives.

Liberals, just as often as conservatives, throw up their hands and condemn positions taken by conservatives by repeating the old cliche themselves: "You have no right to legislate morality." Conservatives in general have advocated laws prohibiting gambling, pornography, drinking, and certain sexual activities such as homosexuality and prostitution.

The desire—and one not to be criticized—is, of course, to improve individual morality. They rarely question how, if we can't legislate morality and improve society by forcing integration, we can make an individual a better person by making him an outlaw if he desires to gamble or drink. The conclusion is that if legislation attempts to improve personal conduct it's okay, but if the aim is to improve economic and social relationships, then it is not.

The failure of those efforts is obvious: prohibition in the 1920's did little to curtail drinking, but did wonders for the growth of the underworld. It also made "criminals" of many Americans.

The comparison to the problem we face today with marijuana is not without merit. Personal morality does not seem to improve with interventionist legislation. Laws prohibiting gambling don't reduce gambling; they just move it to the hands of the underworld figures, limiting it to the bold who break laws and denying it from the law abiders who use it as a form of entertainment.

The strongest criticism directed toward the Moral Majority comes from the pious liberals who condemn it and the like-minded church groups for getting involved in politics and "for legislating morality" on issues involving printed matter, sex habits, and drugs. And yet that's exactly what they have been doing themselves for decades. When the shoe is on the other foot, they resort to the same cliche. Certainly both liberals and conservative religious groups have a right to be involved in politics. How can it be argued otherwise? It seems that as soon as someone promotes a viewpoint contrary to another's beliefs, it's condemned as "legislating morality." Every piece of legislation promoted in Washington is done with a moral overtone and done in the name of "moral obligation" to either help certain groups socially and economically or to make others better persons.

Personal morality does not seem to improve with interventionist legislation.

If it is true that all good law is based on moral principles, how can this impasse occur? Shall we arbitrarily choose when to use "morality" in legislation, based on our own subjective feelings and personal biases?

I believe that's exactly what we've been doing for fifty-to-sixty years, and it has led us to the predicament we face today with most constitutional restraints on government power being removed. It is indeed critical to have a proper understanding of the relationship of morality and the law. Liberals and conservatives can't both be right, and it could hardly be argued that morality is unrelated to the legislative process. Could it be that they are both wrong and both right?

The case is easily made that good law is law based on morality. Is it not obviously immoral to kill, to steal, to assault another, or to defraud? Is it not clearly a moral right to speak one's thoughts, to write, and to practice one's religion, while recognizing slander, libel, breaking of contracts, inciting to riot, and using force to compel one to follow a certain religious belief to be immoral and thus within the scope of the law?

If this is the case—that all worthwhile law is clearly based on a moral code—how can it be correct that liberals should not "legislate morality," use government to feed the poor, and compel intolerant people to reject prejudice and bigotry, as sincere conservatives claim? Likewise, how can the liberals be correct when they chastise the conservative moralists for legislating morality or personal conduct such as gambling, drinking, pornography, and sexual behavior?

Indeed all law, if decent and just, is moral. Morality must guide legislation or it has no meaning whatsoever. Immoral law is law written by dictators, detractors of freedom, and disciples of ignorance. All good law is based on the moral principle of God-given rights—that our life and liberty are natural and endowed to us by our Creator. All law must be written to protect against any adversary of life and liberty and can never assume that life and liberty somehow have been granted out of graciousness from the state. If this rule were followed, all law would have a correct relationship to morality. This precludes the use of violence or force or the threat of such by individuals, groups, or governments to implement change or to correct less than perfect conditions as perceived subjectively by some. Moral law is law which protects freedom and the right to retain the fruits of one's labor and punishes those who commit violent acts against life or property.

Comments on Moral Law:

1) Moral law deals with interpersonal behavior, providing the prohibitions against acts of violence and the protection of one's life, liberty, and property. It never compels relationships, it only works to prevent

and punish those who abuse the absolute and natural rights of others. Laws against murder, theft, assault, and fraud are clear examples of these prohibitions and are obviously based on morality.

2) Moral law should not be used to legislate a moral code of personal behavior with the intent of making someone a "better" person. Legislation cannot alter habits and personal preferences if these preferences are not violating someone else's life, liberty, or property. Personal conduct should not be controlled by law if this conduct affects no one else. This is not to say that personal habits and conduct are not moral or immoral, just that moral law is neutral in regulating this activity, even if it is self-destructive; i.e., drinking, smoking, or eating oneself to death. Moral philosophers and theologians can preach, dictate, and discuss proper personal moral actions, but moral law cannot. If legislation does, it violates the fundamental principle of moral law—the absolute right of the individual to life, liberty, and property. Legislation should not be used to improve personal moral behavior, nor can it be used to improve social and economic conditions. Using force, no matter how well-intended is never justified in a free society. Yes, this means an individual has the right to be selfish, the right to self-indulgence, and the right to freely choose all associations. Government, through legislation, cannot protect the person from himself or herself and should limit its activities to preventing injuries to others and punish those who violate the rights of others.

3) Violence, or the threat of violence by compelling certain actions, cannot be used to improve interpersonal relationships or social conditions. The use of the political process to redistribute wealth or "improve" social conditions, as perceived by a government planner, must of necessity make use of government threats—taxation and imprisonment—and this cannot be done without violating the moral right of another to his life—the fundamental principle of moral law. All improvement and a higher standard of living must result from the incentive system and profit motive. The victims of tragedies beyond anyone's control must be cared for by voluntary means.

The important point to remember is that, in a free society, productivity is maximized, and the increased wealth available for voluntary distribution assures the least amount of suffering. Under an immoral legal system where force is used for redistribution, even if for well-intended goals, production drops and charity flounders. Clinging to a subsistence level of existence then occupies the time of the majority of people. Where the liberal uses government force in trying to improve social conditions, the conservative uses government force to improve personal conduct. Both are based on the same principle, but neither can be successful, because both sincerely motivated attempts backfire and produce opposite results—one leading to hunger and the other to censorship. Massive numbers of citizens eventually get involved in "criminal" activity by being forced into the underground economy and the secret practice of non-sanctioned activities, such as gambling and drug usage.

Using force, no matter how well-intended is never justified in a free society.

---

4) When personal habits—construed as immoral, but permitted under a legal moral system, such as drinking, gambling, and prostitution—disturb the peace, they can, under these circumstances, be curtailed and should be curtailed by the law. Not because the law judges the personal actions as immoral in the religious sense or makes the acts themselves illegal, but the acts become immoral when they violate another's rights or another's privacy. Under these conditions drinking is legal, drunk driving is not; prostitution is legal, but disrupting a neighborhood is not; pornography in private is legal, but public display of the same is not.

5) Intimidating children and forcing adult decisions on them cannot be an accepted practice. Free choice can hardly be construed to permit an adult to subject a 12-year-old to a high-pressure sales pitch for alcohol, drugs, or cigarettes. It happens that this is more likely to occur with illegal items, such as drugs, than with legal ones. Pushers are more likely to push illegal marijuana than they are to push legal alcohol, due to the artificial profits which accompany dealing with illegal drugs. The use of children in pornography obviously violates the right of the innocent child, with his immaturity in making an adult choice, and deserves protection of the state by prohibiting such acts.

6) If poverty or social suffering come from fraud, coerced labor, or acts of force of any sort, the state's role is to punish and remove the obstacles to free associations. If poverty arises from laziness or tragedy, the state cannot "correct" the problem by becoming a problem, i.e., a participant in the use of force.

7) The government's role in general should be to restrain those committing violent acts and not to compel citizens to act in any prescribed way. Using government tax-collecting powers to "promote the

family," as some conservatives desire, makes no more sense than the redistributive process of the welfare system promoted by the liberals. The error in understanding moral law is the same; the results are different, only because the subjective personal preference of the groups are different. Both liberals and conservatives violate the strict definition of moral law when they attempt to "legislate morality" as they see it.

8) Frequently social problems are made worse than they need to be. Liberals who honestly want to help make the problems worse by using the law perversely; i.e., committing government to violent acts of compulsion and redistribution. Efforts should be made to repeal laws that force on us acts of bigotry. Free-market solutions, such as the voluntary boycott, deserve absolute protection of the law since it was and is a non-violent, voluntary act available to effect constructive change. Usually the need for government intervention arises from the previous overuse or misuse of government power.

Prohibition of alcohol did little to improve individual character and reduce drinking, but did promote criminality by encouraging the growth of the mob who controlled the illegal alcoholic beverages.

9) "Legislating morality" in social, economic, and personal affairs is completely different from making law conform to moral principles." Liberals and conservatives are both right when they say the other should not "legislate morality." Both are wrong when each ignores the fact that law should be based on an overriding moral principle.

Some who agree with this moral principle of law claim it's unimportant to be concerned about individual morality and social problems. This is not so. What is important is that the moral principle on which the law rests should not be violated in effecting change. If force is used in an attempt to make people in society moral, it destroys the law. Restraining those who initiate force makes the law moral. Making people moral or society better can only come about by persuasion, and not compulsion, and should be a concern of all decent people. Any attempt by liberals and conservatives to make people and society moral through coercion destroys moral law.

10) It might be asked why a limited use of government to improve the individual and society might not be acceptable; i.e., prohibit gambling and drinking and use government force to feed and care for only the truly needy? Many Americans assume that it is possible to regulate gambling and drinking but not eating habits, feed the poor, but not the lazy. In theory, if human nature is ignored, it could occur. When we allow the seeds of government intervention to be sown, they

grow and spread as bad weeds do in an unattended garden, destroying the useful crop. Once this authority is granted, even if intended to be of limited scope, it eats away at the roots of natural rights and at the principle of sovereignty of the people. Even a small concession leads to an ultimate attack on all individual rights, for there is no logical or consistent argument to oppose the expansion of government power. The process may proceed slowly at first, but eventually the entire system will crumble due to the inevitable "root-rot" that will develop. That is what we are seeing today.

Moral Law or Legislated Morality

It is correct to say: "We cannot legislate morality." But it is also correct to say: "All good legislation is based on a strict moral principle". Laws can never make people better or compel people to be socially responsible. Good legislation, however, is consistent with the moral principle of the natural and God-given right to our lives, our liberty, and our property. Conservatives and liberals misuse the law when they attempt to use it to improve people or society at the expense of the moral commitment to individual God-given rights.

The Founding Fathers understood God-given rights and presented us with the most extraordinary political document ever known in history—our Constitution. This set of laws demonstrated a moral commitment to liberty and was written principally to establish once and for all a new concept—that sovereignty shall be placed in the hands of the people—not in the power of the state. For this reason, the Constitution's entire theme is the limitation of government power—prohibiting the government and the law from being a social and economic planner or individual moralist.

The Founding Fathers did not advocate "legislating morality," but they did outline a legal framework based on a deep moral commitment to the principle that the life and liberty of everyone are gifts of the Creator and not a grant from the state. The purpose of the law to them was to protect life and liberty from the foreign invader, the gangster, the embezzler, the bureaucrat, and the politically ambitious. This concept of morality and law could serve us well, but the conflict between those "legislating morality" for various reasons—such as those who want to improve social and economic conditions and those who want to make people better—will end in social upheaval and the total destruction of the moral foundation on which a free society is built.

The two, "moral law" and "legislating morality," cannot exist together. One ultimately replaces the other. Today, we are in a transition, and the battle is becoming more vicious as social and economic conditions and personal morality worsen. Each side blames the other, but each compounds the error by responding with more bold and enthusiastic attempts at "moral legislation."

Although our experience with a Constitution which was committed to moral law was unique and successful, many leaders pursue and continue to drag us down the path toward a tyrannical state. The battle to determine the final outcome between these opposing forces is now in process. The odds of our losing the concept of moral law and of the "legislators of morality" winning are great. Throughout history, the tyrants—those who know what's best for everybody else, whether it's social or personal—have generally been in charge. I believe, though, with the correct efforts being made and with commitment to understanding our Constitution, our country can survive intact. The 1980's should tell us this.

Definition of Individual Rights

If a precise understanding of rights is not generally agreed upon, a political system designed to protect individual liberty cannot be achieved. The signers of the Declaration of Independence declared that rights are inalienable; i.e., incapable of being lost or surrendered. To avoid any misunderstanding, something this important must be clearly defined. Lincoln pointed out the danger of a vague definition when he said:

> The world has never had a good definition of the word liberty, and the American people, just now, are much in want of one. We all declare for liberty, but in using the same word, we do not all mean the same thing. With some the word liberty means for each man to do as he pleases with himself and the product of his labor; while with others the same word may mean for some men to do as they please with other men, and the products of other men's labor. Here are two, not only different, but incompatible things called by the same name—liberty. It follows that each of the things is, by the

> perceptive parties, called by two different and incompatible names—liberty and tyranny.

The world today, just as in Lincoln's time, is still in need of a good definition for the word liberty. But more than that, we need determined people who believe in and are willing to defend liberty.

Those who dare to use the word liberty when promoting violence and tyranny must be clearly exposed. The tyrants must be identified and never confused as friends of freedom. If a battle must occur—which

---

The world today, just as in Lincoln's time, is still in need of a good definition for the word liberty.

---

inevitably it must since liberty and tyranny cannot coexist—let it never be supposed that two factions advocating liberty are battling one another. The conflict must be clearly between liberty and tyranny.

In order to minimize the confusion, we must do our best to define rights. A right is a natural or God-given permit received at birth, to act in one's own self-interest with total control over one's own life and property as long as others are not injured nor their property taken or damaged. Liberty does not come as a grant from the state. The state can only expect those funds from the individual required to guarantee that the rights of all are equally protected. Ideally those funds would be collected through a voluntary agreement between the state and each citizen. The role of the government in a free society is limited to settling disputes when the voluntary courts fail. Minimal police activity is warranted when private security falters. The protection of our geographic borders providing adequate national security from outside threats is a proper function of a government dedicated to protecting individual freedom.

Individuals in a free society must have the right to keep the fruits of their labor if the concept of individual rights is to have any meaning.

There is no conflict between what is called "natural" rights and "God-given" rights. The Founding Fathers said we were endowed by our "Creator" with our rights, but they also had no qualms with the term natural rights. It certainly seems reasonable that life and liberty come as a magnificent gift from the Creator. Obviously it cannot come from a government official, an act of Congress, the Constitution, the Declaration of Independence, or the Magna Carta. Quite to the contrary, tragically governments over the centuries have done a lot more to destroy this natural gift than they have to secure it.

I see no conflict between the self "ownership" concept associated with natural rights and those who, for religious reasons, believe their life is "owned" by God. One is a political concept and the other a religious concept. Obviously no one can dictate another's religious belief. What one does with one's life and property is a personal decision and it may or may not include religious beliefs. In a free society a person can "turn his life over to God" or squander it as he chooses. The important thing is that the state not be permitted to assume any ownership role of the individual.

A society built on the principle of individual rights rejects the notion that the state should protect a citizen from himself. Government cannot and should not protect against one's own "unwise" decisions. Freedom is impossible once a government assumes a role in regulating the people's eating, sleeping, drinking, smoking, and exercise habits. Once government believes it has an obligation to improve or protect the people physically, it will then claim it can protect them economically and intellectually. It leads to a regimented society, hostile to individuals who cling to the notion that their lives and liberty are their own. Conservatives certainly must be reminded that "civil" liberty is the same as economic liberty, and present-day liberals must be told that economic liberty deserves the same protection that the written and spoken word get under the First Amendment. Preemptive regulations of either literary or commercial activity, for any reason, are prohibited in a free society. Fraud and libel are crimes that, when proven in a court of law, must be punished.

The most important element of a free society, where individual rights are held in the highest esteem, is the rejection of the initiation of violence. All initiation of force is a violation of someone else's rights, whether initiated by an individual or the state, for the benefit of an individual or group of individuals, even if it's supposed to be for the benefit of another individual or group of individuals. Legitimate use of violence can only be that which is required in self-defense.

This means that all associations are voluntary and by mutual consent of both parties. Contracts drawn up without force or fraud must be rigidly adhered to. This sounds reasonable, and most people would agree with this outline of mutually agreed-to associations. But it also means that free people have the right to discriminate—in choosing a spouse, a friend, a business partner, an employer, an employee, a customer, etc.

Civil rights legislation of the past thirty years has totally ignored this principle. Many "do-gooders," of course, argue from the "moral high ground" for their version of equal rights, knowing that they can play on the sympathies and the guilt of many Americans. Yet the real reason for some of these laws is less than noble. For instance, minimum wage laws are popular, but the proponents rarely admit that this protects higher-paid union jobs and increases unemployment.

Total freedom of contract and association is what the "pursuit of happiness" is all about. Once this principle is violated, the gradual but steady erosion of our liberties can be expected unless the principle of individual rights is reestablished.

Free choice means that the incentive to produce is maximized, since it's assumed that we can keep the fruits of our labor. In a free society, an individual benefits from wise and frugal decisions and suffers the consequences of bad judgment and wasteful habits. The state should neither guarantee nor tax success, nor compensate those who fail. The individual must be responsible for all of his decisions. Because some suffer from acts outside of their control, we cannot justify the use of violence to take from someone else to "help out." People in need are not excused when they rob their neighbors, and government should not be excused when it does the robbing for them. Providing for the general welfare means that the general conditions of freedom must be maintained. It should never be used to justify specific welfare or any transfer of wealth from one person to another.

A free society permits narrow self-interest but allows for compassion and self-sacrifice. Greed, when associated with force or fraud, is not acceptable. A free society is more likely to survive if compassion is voluntarily shown for the unfortunate than if the poor are ignored. A healthy self-interest associated with a sense of responsibility for family and friends is far superior to a welfare state built on foolish self-sacrifice and violent redistribution of wealth.

A society that holds in high esteem the principle of individual rights is superior in all ways to a society that distorts the meaning of liberty and condones the use of government coercion.

CHAPTER II

Foreign Policy

The proper concept of individual rights is the most fundamental ingredient of a free society. Nearly as important to a country is foreign policy. An unwise foreign policy leads to unnecessary violence and death on a massive scale. A society built on the concept of individual rights will logically have a foreign policy of nonintervention. It is important to understand what this involves and what happens when foreign entanglements are easily entered.

Throughout the twentieth century, the United States has steadily drifted from the traditional policy of nonintervention, neutrality, and independence to one of interventionism in the internal affairs of other nations, covert foreign activity, and broad international commitments.

This dramatic shift in policy, one of the major U. S. blunders of this century, is responsible for all of our overseas military conflicts of the past eight decades, which have resulted in more than 650,000 Americans killed and 1,130,000 Americans wounded. The last two major conflicts, Korea and Vietnam, were fought without a formal declaration of war. In modern language, they were "police actions." Since war was not declared, there was no commitment to win. Clearly the efforts proved futile, serving only to tear at the seams of American society.

Policy shifts have since occurred, but reassessment of the overall foreign intervention policy has not taken place. Reassessment must occur if the senseless killing is to be stopped.

Many who frowned upon the Libyan bombing and the Grenada invasion did not do so from a principled position of nonintervention. And some who criticized the invasion of Grenada were supportive of the Libyan bombing. The only current debate is which faction of interventionism will be supported—fascist or communist dictators.

A trend toward internationalism worldwide has characterized this century; the fact that some call the twentieth century the "bloody century" is not just coincidental. During this century, 35,000,000 people have been killed in war, but totalitarian regimes have murdered an additional 119,000,000 people. And we worry about a nuclear holocaust! Modern weaponry certainly can be blamed for a great deal of the massive destruction of modern war, but the collectivist ideology that breeds totalitarianism is the root cause. Our job as concerned citizens of a free society is to do everything in our power to deter our own participation in the ghoulish killing.

Following the constitutional intent of the Founding Fathers would go a long way in achieving this goal.

The Constitution and Foreign Policy

The Constitution never mentions the term "foreign policy," but today it is routinely heard that the Constitution grants the power to conduct foreign policy exclusively to the President.

It is also frequently heard in Congress, especially when foreign entanglements get serious, that we must fall in line and support a nonpartisan policy. In other words, they argue, there should be no real debate on what is going on when it comes to foreign policy.

Opposition to our involvement in the major conflicts of this century have elicited cries of treason for not supporting the consensus position. But if the Constitution is closely studied, one finds that the Founding Fathers never intended the President to assume total control over foreign affairs.

The President clearly was granted power "to make treaties...appoint ambassadors, other public ministers, and consuls," but only with the advice and consent of the Senate. Two-thirds of the Senate must concur to ratify a treaty, whereas a majority can confirm an appointment. Clearly, the President is made the Commander-in-Chief of the military.

Nothing is said about monopoly power to pursue policy that involves invasion, intrigue, murder, blockades, conspiracy, and funding of foreign powers that has characterized the twentieth century.

The Congress, in contrast, was given much more say over foreign policy. The Congress is instructed to:

> ...provide for the common defense and general welfare of the United States...; to define and punish piracies and felonies committed on the high seas, and offenses against the laws of nations; to declare war, grant letters of marque and reprisal, and make rules concerning captures on land and water; to raise and support armies...; to pursue and maintain a navy; to make rules for the government and regulation of the land and naval forces; to provide for calling up the militia, to execute the laws of the union, suppress insurrections and repel invasion; to provide for organizing, arming, and disciplining the militia, and for governing such part of them as may be employed in the service of the United States....

In comparison, it is quite apparent that the Founding Fathers placed a greater trust in the people acting through Congress in determining precise policy. The President cannot declare war; therefore, he is not permitted, according to the Constitution, to wage war without the vote of Congress; and he has no authority to spend any money on foreign adventurism without the consent of Congress. Even treaties and appointments are only permissible after congressional approval.

Obviously the Founding Fathers feared a strong and aggressive presidency when it came to foreign and military affairs. The President is certainly the Commander-in-Chief of the military, fulfilling the desire of the Founding Fathers of guaranteeing civilian control over the military, but the idea of the military was that of having sufficient military strength to repel an invasion and defend the country. If it required calling up the militia, which only Congress was authorized to do, the President would be in charge of the military operations. It is impossible to argue from a constitutional viewpoint, that involvement in any conflict is the prerogative of the President.

This careless notion, so frequently repeated, that the President is in total charge of foreign policy, cannot be justified by anything read in the Constitution. Congress has the major responsibility for any foreign commitment.

It is now up to the people to reclaim this right, by insisting upon representation reflecting the people's views, not the narrow view of the special interests who have benefited from both our military and economic intervention of the past eighty years.

Obviously the Founding Fathers feared a strong and aggressive presidency when it came to foreign and military affairs.

So often when objections to our foreign policies are finally heard, they are only for partisan or special-interest reasons. Rarely are these objections due to deeply held philosophic reasons grounded in constitutional history.

Because the politicians in this century have not followed the traditional policy of the Founding Fathers for avoiding foreign entanglements, America has suffered the consequences. We can expect continued foreign military conflicts, hostage crises, and terrorist attacks that solve nothing, while killing and maiming innocent Americans and our draft-age youth, until a policy of nonintervention is once again accepted as proper and wise.

Acceptance in America

When America became careless about defining the purpose of government, foreign policy changed. Guaranteeing the inalienable rights of individuals should be the prime role of government, and national sovereignty is recognized as proper for this purpose.

However, once this goal of guaranteeing and protecting the individual becomes muddled, as it certainly has, vague reasons are given for the existence of the state. Behind all the muddle is usually the age-old temptation of some to use power to control others.

This is done in moral terms by claiming that the needs of others are the concern of us all. Likewise, the goal of achieving international power, both financial and military, is done with moral overtones—such as "making the world safe for democracy." Foreign aid—although its real purpose is to enhance the riches of foreign dictators, international bankers, and some American industrialists—is pawned off as aid to the people of the impoverished Third World.

This philosophy of internationalism has lead to a tremendous growth in foreign welfare, especially since 1945, and a foreign policy of internationalism that has virtually removed the sovereign conviction of guaranteeing the individual rights of American citizens. Instead of making the world safe for democracy, a goal set by Woodrow Wilson, the world is no longer safe, especially for American citizens traveling abroad.

The combination of liberalism's naive belief that the world can be made a better place through socialist redistribution of wealth and the desire of certain international bankers to control the world through one-world government has brought us to a dangerous period in our history. Today the proposals of the Council of Foreign Relations and the Trilateral Commission have much more impact on policy than the Constitution. Sadly, world socialist order is of prime concern, not individual liberty, as it should be. This mixture of misplaced liberal idealism and the bankers' goal of world domination, forces capitalists and communists to do business together on many occasions.

Many American arms manufacturers, as well as other "Rambo" Americans, have an insatiable hunger to perpetually have a fearsome enemy. Therefore, on the surface, it always looks like we are about to go to war with the Soviets while, behind the scenes, we continue to fund the very enemy who "threatens" to invade our hemisphere.

Internationalism is enhanced by this war-monger policy, and individual liberty is diminished. The Constitution is forgotten, as is the traditional American foreign policy practiced for more than a hundred years of minding our own business and providing security for America.

It is bad enough to see the loss of liberty for which the Founding Fathers fought so valiantly, but to watch a foreign policy that has led to perpetual war for America presents a great danger to us all.

Errors Compound

Just as with economic interventionism, each government action in the affairs of other nations causes more problems than it solves. Instead of achieving peace, perpetual conflict occurs. Instead of expressing gratitude for our foreign largesse, the recipients of American aid become resentful. Instead of achieving a greater national security, America becomes more vulnerable and weak.

The odds of getting assistance from our allies to protect our security if we are threatened are infinitesimal, as compared to the possibility of our sons dying for someone else's security. The odds of our being involved unnecessarily in another unwise foreign military venture continues.

Johnathan Kwitny, in *Endless Enemies*, documents numerous occasions when our intervention has led to a failed military operation and hostility toward America. In contrast, he demonstrates that when we pursued a neutralist course, our interests were better served, relationships were better, and it cost the American taxpayers a lot less.

Sadly the debate is never between a constitutional foreign policy and interventionism; it is clearly a debate between factions of interventionism. Both sides assume great wisdom and propose solutions to the problems of the world, while ignoring American security and the right of her citizens. However, the public justification for all U.S. intervention is that this intervention benefits the American citizen.

The conservatives argue continually for *more* military expenditures and aid to the anti-communist regime; the liberals argue for *less* total military spending, but plenty of aid for the pro-communist nations.

Members of Congress generally accept that there are only two options available to us, refusing to admit that these options are only variations of a single interventionist foreign policy. Our goal should be to make certain that a third option, the constitutional principle of nonintervention, is emphatically heard in the debate.

Since we can never get a consensus of which faction to support in other nations, one group of Americans is unjustly forced to subsidize the other's preferences. If the purpose were only to serve the direct interests of American citizens in our homeland, the whole discussion would never arise. There is no reason to force the liberal to finance Somosa or the conservative, the Sandanistas. Securing peace, preserving liberty, and protecting the life and property of American citizens are the only legitimate functions of government equally beneficial to all. It should be, for that reason, noncontroversial.

Not only is it unfair to pass on the cost of meddling in the affairs of other nations to the citizens who disagree with the policies pursued, when intervention leads to hostilities, the commitments involved are very serious indeed.

Literally, we put the lives of our youth and the youth of future generations on the line. There is no moral justification for this. Military treaties obligate future generations to commitments that only individuals of that generation should fulfill.

We should reassess all our military treaties. They are called "mutual security" treaties, but no one expects our allies to come to our assistance if we are attacked. Events in Korea, Vietnam, Libya, and Iran show how insignificant the support is that we get from our allies. We have been forced to stand alone and bear all the cost of our defense and most of the cost of the defense of our allies.

There is no moral justification for one generation's committing another generation to pay higher taxes, to suffer more inflation, to sacrifice the lives of their youth (uprooted through conscription) for needless armed conflicts. With a noninterventionist foreign policy, citizens would never be forced to subsidize or die for any special interest. Taxes could be used only to secure peace and freedom for America.

Under these conditions of nonintervention, of course, individuals would never be prohibited from volunteering and contributing their own monies to any foreign cause. Our government is the only legal dealer in weapons of war, usually at a high cost to American taxpayers, as well as danger to our security. Thus the wishes of citizens are violated with every transaction. Americans who want to privately help anti-communists in Cuba, Afghanistan, El Salvador, or Nicaragua should be free to do so, and yet they are not.

The first major change in our foreign policy occurred at the turn of the century. President McKinley initiated the change leading us into the Spanish-American War. Woodrow Wilson made the most radical departure from our traditional noninterventionist foreign policy; he sought to:

> ...make the world safe for democracy...America's duty is to stand shoulder-to-shoulder to lift the burdens of mankind in the future, and show the path of freedom to all the world. The American flag is henceforth to stand for self-possession, for dignity, and for the assertion of the right of one nation to serve other nations of the world. America is now rich enough and free enough to look abroad for great tasks to perform. Our duty is to serve the world.

The idea that it is our government's duty to serve the world and that we have great tasks to perform throughout the world, is an example of an outrageous and irrational idealism.

Even though World War I was the first major break from our traditional position of nonintervention, the Spanish-American War conditioned our people to accept our new role as world police.

Walter Karp, in his outstanding work *The Politics of War*, points out that "it was the very alliance that Republicans had forged with Wall

Street which required the protection of war and a forward foreign policy." Karp describes vividly how our new-found interventionist policy maneuvered us into the unnecessary Spanish-American War.

Karp, in his book, also describes our involvement in World War I and Wilson's participation with tremendous skill. Although most of us have been taught that Woodrow Wilson was one of our five great Presidents, it is unlikely that one would come to this conclusion after reading this book. Karp documents how Wilson maneuvered us into World War I in 1917. Wilson's grandiose assumption that he could "make the world safe for democracy" and fulfill our "duty to serve the world" prompted the wounding and killing of hundreds of thousands of young American soldiers, bringing needless sorrow to millions of American families.

Not only is this maneuvering into war a horror, Karp's description of how Wilson suspended personal freedoms at home, an inevitable consequence of war-mongering, is frightening.

In times of war, personal freedoms are threatened at home.

In times of war, personal freedoms are threatened at home. That is why a proper foreign policy is so critical: so that freedoms at home are never again threatened. We have been able to recover some of the freedoms taken from us in times of war, but the real danger is that someday—under war conditions, preparation for war, or economic chaos brought on by inflation—our freedoms will be permanently lost.

Wilson once wrote that the sovereignty of the American people was "...a mere legal fiction." Personal liberty was *a mere legal fiction* to Wilson as well.

Twenty-three years after World War I ended, America entered the Second World War, largely as a consequence of Franklin Roosevelt's interventionist foreign policy. An excellent description of this can be found in Charles Callan Tansill's *Back Door to War*. From this outstanding historic documentation of what transpired prior to the war, it is clear that the United States deliberately provoked the Japanese into attacking Pearl Harbor for economic reasons. Since the United States had broken the Japanese code, Roosevelt knew exactly what the Japanese were planning. FDR did nothing because of his own political ambitions and his desire to unify the country in support of the war. By the early 1940's only a small minority stood on principle and objected to our becoming allies with Soviet murderers.

Our role as international police became an accepted fact when the policy of internationalism, enhanced by our United Nations membership, involved us in Korea and Vietnam as the result of treaty obligations. This policy ignored and denied the rights to life and liberty of the young men who were maimed or tragically killed. The Korean and Vietnam Wars were conducted without even asking for congressional approval.

The policy of compulsive meddling worldwide has created nothing but trouble and confusion for America. The most recent scandal, involving weapons to Iran for the release of hostages and the secret and illegal funding of the Contras in Nicaragua, is a perfect example of how foolish the policy of interventionism can be.

For years American taxpayers were forced to subsidize the Shah under the pretense that America's security depended upon it. The truth is that this funding protected privileged business interests in Iran. With the overthrow of the Shah, all this changed. The taking of American hostages by the Iranians and the failure of Carter to secure their release was the major reason Carter lost so badly in 1980 to Ronald Reagan.

Our announced policy toward the Iran-Iraq War is one of neutrality. But now we find, and it really should be to no one's surprise, that we have been aiding both Iraq and Iran. Our government leaders maneuver continuously to remain in a position of influence, regardless of which faction controls a foreign nation, friend or foe, so that the interests of the bankers and certain industrialists will be served.

Those who insist that we must "protect" Iran from the Soviets never explain why the concern is so great when we see the miserable failure of the Soviet military machine in neighboring Afghanistan. Nor is it explained why we now are allies of the Soviets in support of Iraq.

The Middle East, in the last forty years, has soaked up billions of dollars in the name of American security and peace. The more we give Israel, the more we must give their Arab enemies.

The height of this folly was vividly and tragically dramatized on October 23, 1981, with the killing of the 241 Marines in Beirut when their barracks were destroyed by radical Moslems. The terrorists probably were aided by Iran and supplied with explosives sold to them by Israel, originating from the United States and paid for by American taxpayers.

The epitome of our bungling foreign policy was revealed when it became known that the Marines standing guard had rifles but were permitted no ammunition because it was thought that any careless killing could precipitate a crisis. Others argued that they were not permitted ammunition because they were incapable of handling their rifles. These absurdities boggle the mind, and yet the American people did little to put an end to it.

This senseless loss of life did nothing to prompt the reassessment of our foreign policy. Instead it led to a sure victory over the "aggressive" military power of Grenada—made up of 200 military personnel. The American people, unfortunately, could not see that both actions were the result of the same flawed policy. The Grenada invasion was heralded as a great triumph and applauded by the vast majority of American people. The truth is that neither the medical students nor the administrator of the medical school ever requested the rescue. The military argument for invasion was shallow. If the airbase in Grenada ever became a threat to the United States, a single missile fired from a ship offshore could destroy it in minutes.

An interesting briefing occurred at the height of the Grenada crisis. Our State Department met in closed session with the Republican members of Congress, including myself, on the day after the invasion. Two political messages emerged from the meeting: one, make sure the administrator of the hospital makes no more public statements that do not show strong support for the rescue mission; and two, have some students express gratitude by kissing the ground on their return to the United States. The next day the tone of the administrator changed as he publicly expressed support for the rescue mission and, amazingly, a few students responded on arrival to the United States by kissing the ground.

The overwhelming "victory" in Grenada was less than a brilliant military operation. There were no Cuban troops of any significance. The landing was changed from 2 a.m. to 5:30 a.m. because the U.S. authorities were uncertain of night operations. Nineteen U.S. soldiers were killed—seven by friendly fire.

The invasion of Grenada is hardly the victory the American people were led to believe.

Extremely poor communications between the branches of the military were encountered. The press reported that one U.S. commander could not get through to his superior and ended up using his credit card to call Ft. Bragg for help. Intelligence reports were faulty and were of no practical use to the invasion.

Worst of all, and typical of our tragic foreign policy—in the midst of the Grenada invasion designed to make the world safe for democracy by stopping the spread of communism—President Reagan, behind the scenes, was forcefully lobbying for specific aid to "Communist-dictators" through additional IMF funding.

The invasion of Grenada is hardly the victory the American people were led to believe.

The United States supported the 1982 Israeli invasion of Lebanon with the relentless bombing of Beirut. While the bombs were still falling on Beirut, a foreign aid bill was brought to the House floor. Aid to Lebanon, at the request of the Administration, was tripled so that Beirut could be rebuilt for "humanitarian reasons." Here we were, already appropriating more money to rebuild the devastated cities destroyed by bombs for which Americans had also paid. This surely was a policy of madness! During this period of time Israel captured 400 Lebanese Moslems and has since then illegally held them in captivity—one of the major reasons for the ongoing hostage crisis we still face.

In 1985 the worst terrorist act occurred in Beirut which killed 80 and injured 200 innocent people. Reliable evidence proves that the act was carried out by a Lebanese intelligence unit trained and supported by our CIA. Their goal and mission was to kill a Shiite leader suspected of terrorizing the U.S. installations.

Our involvement in the Middle East has also contributed indirectly to the deaths of 248 soldiers in an aircraft accident in which a DC-8 crashed in Gander, Newfoundland, in December 1985. The plane was returning from the Gaza strip, on Israel's southern border, where soldiers had been serving on a peace-keeping mission for the United Nations. The aircraft accident investigation panel revealed direct causes to be: a failure to de-ice, overweight, and a power failure. The aircraft was leased from a fly-by-night charter airline to *save money.* Unbelievably we spend $300 billion a year on national defense (or *foreign meddling*) and we cannot afford decent aircraft to transport our troops. A policy designed to guarantee American security would never permit such senseless tragedies.

The U.S. policy toward Libya further confirms our irrational foreign policy. Under Reagan we have been determined to pick a fight with Khadafi, defying him with naval and air maneuvers in the Gulf of Sidra. As we try to emphasize our right to navigate in international waters near Libya, we totally reject the territorial waters of Nicaragua by mining their harbors. The World Court rulings against the U.S. were ignored by the Reagan Administration, yet the President insists that international law is legitimate in the Gulf of Sidra. The most important point, however, is that the Gulf of Sidra has *nothing* to do with U.S. security.

The bombing of Libya while sending arms to Iran—who has been much more involved in international terrorism—reveals the schizophrenic nature of our foreign policy.

Bombing a foreign capital, and killing innocent civilians, including a young daughter of Khadafi—even if the opinion polls support the action—*is* an act of war and *not* authorized by our Constitution. Action of this sort cannot be construed as necessary to protect American security. The bombing was, however, an historic first—it was scheduled in time for the evening news in the United States!

The bombing can hardly be considered a military success. Of the 18 F-111's deployed, only 11 completed the mission; one was shot down. Thirty-eight percent of the planes could not fly the 2800 miles over undefended territory. The craziness of flying such a distance (10 hours roundtrip), when the same mission could have been accomplished more effectively from aircraft carriers, can only be explained by the desire to give the Air Force a little "glory" as well as the Navy. Others have argued that the reason for the long flight was to force our allies to "fish or cut bait" with our policy on terrorism.

It is interesting to note that after forty years of massive foreign aid to Europe, of hundreds of billions of dollars, both military and economic, our allies "cut bait." We received no assistance from Greece, Germany, Italy, Spain, Turkey, or France. Some investment!

All this expense (which added nothing to our defense and made us more vulnerable) for allies who couldn't care less. Instead of pressuring the allies to go along with some of our extravagant involvements overseas, *we* need to "cut bait" and leave Europe and the Middle East. We'd be a lot safer and richer for it.

The sad part about our bombing Libya is that a tin-horn dictator has caused America to betray her principles. In an effort to gain support for "getting Khadafi," a deliberate government campaign of disinformation was carried out. This campaign was similar to the disinformation that led to the Gulf of Tonken resolution and the subsequent killing of 60,000 American soldiers in Vietnam.

This "Rambo" attitude of our politicians reflects the insecurity and loss of confidence in ourselves. It does not reflect a positive American patriotism like some would have us believe. American patriotism should reflect a positive belief in freedom and prompt actions that guarantee individual liberty.

If motivated by American patriotism, government action would have been different in the Miroslav Medvid affair. Medvid is the Russian sailor, who jumped the Russian freighter in October 1985 as it sailed up the Mississippi. When the United States authorities were returning him to the Soviet vessel, he again leapt out of the U.S. Border Patrol boat. He was captured and, under great duress, was again forced to return to the Russian vessel. The United States officials told the public that Medvid "changed his mind and wanted to go back." The U.S. interpreter, however, disagreed and said Medvid sincerely sought freedom. A positive conviction of American patriotism would have prompted quite a different response from us.

The ironies of our foreign policy are endless. We have troops in over 120 countries of the world and support, financially and militarily, *both* sides of most of the current military conflicts.

Our politicians' enthusiasm for foreign aid is not shared by a majority of the American people, nor does it conform to the Constitution. It is frequently justified by a flawed understanding of the Marshall Plan. The $1.7 billion foreign aid gift to Western Europe between 1948 and 1952 is usually given the credit for European recovery after the War. Under occupation from 1945-1948, the economy of Europe remained weak and the Marshall Plan coincided with some policy changes. An imposed economic policy by the United States on Europe between 1945 and 1948 kept the economy weak. But in June 1948 Ludwig Erhard abolished all Allied economic controls and devalued and stabilized the German mark, and the economy surged. Because foreign aid arrived at the same time, American politicians have demanded the credit and used this program to perpetuate this technique of serving some American businesses and banking interests.

In reality, the Marshall Plan never contributed to more than five percent of one European country's gross national product, while occupational cost remained at fifteen percent. This subsidy was minuscule compared to the economic growth statistics of the 1950's. The argument that a dollar shortage existed in Europe and an injection of funds was needed is an old Keynesian argument used to justify foreign-aid expenditures. The bad policies of inflation and economic control, imposed by the U.S. after the war were the real culprits. In contrast to the argument that the Marshall Plan was market-oriented, we find (under close scrutiny) the rules discouraged free enterprise, served the special interests of some American industries, and did nothing to enhance free trade with the other Western nations.

There are other numerous absurdities that have resulted from our foreign policy:

Corazon Aquino in 1986, addressed the U.S. Congress. The speech was so impressive that within hours the House voted $150 million in additional aid to the Philippines. Aquino responded by saying, "It wasn't enough."

Marcos received billions from us over the years with no accounting or control of expenditures. The question no one can answer is how the Philippines have made us more secure in the last thirty years.

After the bombing of Libya, Khadafi's navy responded by bombarding the island of Lampedusa in the Mediterranean. It was then that we discovered we had U.S. Coast Guard personnel on this island—guarding our coastline, I guess.

We have 340,000 troops in Europe and over 200,000 elsewhere around the world. It costs $140 billion a year to protect Europe and $50 billion a year to defend Japan. It costs approximately $1000 to maintain each man per day overseas. This assistance permits a competitive edge for our allies, who are well ahead of us technologically, and contributes to our trade deficit. Our only response has been to promote protectionism, making the problem worse. Overall foreign policy has never been seriously considered as the basic flaw, like it someday must.

We placed economic sanctions on South Africa at precisely the same time President Reagan approved subsidized wheat sales to the Soviets. The sanctions were a liberal political stunt; the subsidies to the Soviet Union were meant to help U.S. wheat farmers and secure the election of the Republican Senate—which it did not. While bombing Libya to deter terrorism, we negotiated with Syria and acted as partners with Israel in its massive ongoing arms trade.

The CIA, not known for its intelligence-gathering skills, has 16,000 agents—2,500 added under William Casey and two-thirds added during the last decade. This agency is only 40 years old and its activities, which include clandestine and ruthless intervention in the affairs of other nations, is neither morally nor constitutionally justified.

Author Dan Smoot, in a letter to me, stated,

> There is no place in a governmental system of a constitutional republic for an agency that meddles in the affairs of foreign nations. Even if the CIA were in the hands of patriots whom I like, I would still feel, as I have felt since 1946, that it should not be. Whatever seeds such an agency sows, the harvest will be detrimental to our nation.

Dan Smoot is a brilliant constitutionalist and a student of history. His fears of the CIA have been legitimate as we continue to see the disastrous results of the CIA involvement around the world.

The National Security Council (NSC) was set up in 1946 to coordinate and advise the President on foreign affairs. The National Security Council was never meant to carry out activities along with the CIA as revealed by the Iran-Contra scandal. It is ironic now to see the appointment of David Abshire to a Cabinet-level post to "coordinate the effort" to resolve the confusion the scandal concocted by the NSC has caused. The one net benefit from the Iran-Contra scandal has been the derailing of a dangerously aggressive foreign policy, clandestinely orchestrated by the CIA.

Not only has our twentieth-century foreign policy failed, it continues to be a serious threat to all of us. It has contributed significantly to our national bankruptcy and has done nothing to enhance our national security. Reevaluation is a must.

A foreign policy of nonintervention should be a topic of serious debate in 1987-1988, the 200th Anniversary of our Constitution. It is an opportune time to consider the reinstatement of a principled noninterventionist American foreign policy.

Noninterventionist Foreign Policy

A noninterventionist foreign policy is both morally and constitutionally correct. From George Washington to Grover Cleveland, this principle was upheld. The twentieth century has been witness to a complete reversal of this policy and millions have suffered as a consequence. Our foolish foreign policy contributes significantly to our national bankruptcy and presents a threat to our national security.

Foreign-policy options of the conservatives and the liberals are, in reality, only a variation of a single interventionist policy. It is only the direction of the intervention that is different and open to debate. Another option must be made available from which the American people may choose.

The policy of neutrality is morally correct for major world powers as well as small nations. By what authority does any country interfere in the internal affairs of another? When a major power interferes, it literally becomes a bully. The excuse for intervention is usually in moralistic terms, arguing that it is for the benefit of the world or a policy of making the world "safe for democracy" and for the purpose of making poor nations prosperous. These are excuses, not reasons based on morality.

What is done in the name of national security is a disgrace and the worst kind of disinformation conceivable.

Officially, getting openly involved in the internal affairs of other nations is always at the host country's request. Those interfering claim they do so by popular support, but the people are never consulted. Our foreign aid goes either to fascist or socialist nations, benefiting the rulers by solidifying their power and impeding the development of a free society and a free-market economy.

The outcome of even the best-motivated assistance is usually the opposite of that which was intended. When economic assistance is sent to other nations with the intention of helping the poor, the poor receive a small fraction of what is sent. But the worst part of all this is that the assistance perpetuates the entire system that causes the impoverishment in the first place and makes it more difficult than ever for the people of that country to achieve more liberty.

Even if aid and interference were handled wisely by patriotic Americans, they could not be justified on moral grounds. If we assume that it is proper for the United States government to meddle in any way in the internal affairs of other nations—even if for noble reasons—the door is then opened for the ruthless who could then intervene for the worst reasons—aiding fascism, socialism, or communism or for personal gain. Providing aid to those struggling to be free by first expropriating funds from innocent Americans cannot be justified. Freedom cannot be spread through a policy of force which violates another man's freedom.

When providing assistance, it is logical to expect some national benefit in return. The policies of nations that have received aid obviously have greater significance to us than those who have not received help. If their policies do not conform to the policies of the United States administration in power, threats, and even assisting in coups, are then said to be justified. After a few decades of international intervention, with economic assistance and covert operations for "national security," the noble original purpose is entirely forgotten. The doors are then opened to almost any type of foreign involvement.

Politically, U.S. intervention is justified by claiming it aids American security. But rarely can we see how the foreign activities are of any benefit to the American taxpayers. The Vietnam conflict was lost and yet we are on better terms than ever with the Vietnamese. Castro's thirty-year hold on Cuba has not yet directly affected American security. A plausible argument could be made for our not wanting a Soviet puppet state ninety miles from our shores, but how can an airbase in Grenada or Nicaragua be any more threatening? Our involvement in the four corners of the earth cannot be legitimately justified as necessary for national security. Most Americans do not have the foggiest idea where Chad or Mozambique are located, nor do they see their political system as crucial to our own security. What is done in the name of national security is a disgrace, and the worst kind of disinformation conceivable.

President Reagan put American intervention in a proper perspective. On July 16, 1986, he was asked whether sending helicopters to Bolivia for drug enforcement was in the national interest and he responded: "Anything we do is in the national interest."

This has been the attitude of most of the Presidents during this century, with the possible exceptions of Coolidge and Hoover. Is it any wonder that we are so involved throughout the world? The truth is that our worldwide involvement is unrelated to national security in the strict sense, but rather is a result of a policy of intervention and acceptance of the notion that the military follows U.S. economic interests, providing protection for our international bankers and businessmen.

If foreign policy were based on moral principles, all intervention of our government in the affairs of other nations would cease, no matter how tempting. Foreign policy's purpose should be limited to providing security and insuring peace for America. The only moral justification for an expenditure is for the defense of our nation. A military manned by volunteers helps to avert unwise military foreign involvement. It is time we challenge those who promote our overseas activities and adventures on moral grounds. We have been pursuing a policy based on good intentions and privilege to the special interests for the past several decades, and America's security has greatly suffered. It is time to quit!

It would be better if we heeded the words of Grover Cleveland who stated best the pre-1900 American foreign policy:

> It is the policy of independence favored by our own love of justice and by our own power. It is the policy of peace suitable to our interest. It is the policy of neutrality, rejecting any share in foreign brawls, and ambitions upon other continents, repelling their intrusions here. It is the policy of Monroe and of Washington and of Jefferson: peace, commerce, and honest friendship with all nations; entangling alliances with none.

Instead our twentieth-century politicians have taken a different course:

A noninterventionist foreign policy is frequently attacked as isolationist. Nothing could be further from the truth. The image of a nation walling itself off from the rest of the world is impossible in a free society and, ironically, is exactly what eventually happens under interventionism.

An internationalist foreign policy includes goals of one-world government and international banking with fiat currencies, and this leads to economic isolationism, where nations become more militaristic and nationalistic. Trade wars ensue, and protectionism follows.

A free society, with a noninterventionist foreign policy, protects the rights of its citizens to travel and trade across borders without tariffs or licenses or capital controls, and rejects all special interest subsidies. Immigration is always permissible, and all attempts to curtail the movement of people and currency are rejected.

The ultimate right of a free society is to be able to vote with your feet and to leave freely with your assets.

This freedom of movement of people and goods would encourage the intermingling of people with a natural balance of trade, assuming nations do not participate in the fraud of inflation. We would in no way create a fortress America, or a country isolated; the exact opposite would result.

Our foreign policy should be directed at making our nation secure from any outside threat so our liberty at home may thrive, to avoid war and promote peace. The ultimate victory over fascism and communism must be won in the minds of men and cannot be achieved by an interventionist foreign policy. Ultimately, totalitarianism can only be defeated by a positive freedom philosophy.

By the 1960's, Kennedy acknowledged to what degree we had rejected this position. In his Inaugural Address in 1961 Kennedy stated:

> Let every nation know, whether it wish us well or ill, that we will pay any price, bear any burden, beat any hardship, support any friend, oppose any foe, to assure the survival and the success of liberty. This much we pledge and more...To those peoples in the huts and villages of half the globe struggling to break the bonds of mass misery we pledge our best efforts to help them help themselves, for whatever period is required—not because the Communists may be doing it, not because we seek their votes, but because it is right. If a free society cannot help the many who are poor they cannot save the few who are rich.

This policy of self-sacrifice that Kennedy advocated is a policy that we have essentially followed this entire century. For this reason we have seen hundreds of thousands of Americans needlessly killed and perpetual international conflict. Unless this policy is changed, we can expect more of the same.

General McArthur, however, expressed concern about this policy. He said in 1957:

> Our government has kept us in a perpetual state of fear—kept us in a continuous stampede of patriotic fervor—with the cry of grave national emergency. Always there has been some terrible evil—to gobble us up if we would not blindly rally behind it by furnishing the exuberant funds demanded.

> Yet, in retrospect, those disasters seem never to have happened, seem never to have been quite real.

War, other than for the actual defense of our nation, must be avoided, for it is during wartime that personal and economic freedoms quickly erode. Although we have regained some of our freedoms removed during periods of war, our liberty has gradually eroded during this century. This will continue if we do not make fundamental changes, because another unwise war could spell doom for us, both economically and politically.

A policy based solely on our self-interest is the best policy for the world, because it encourages a proper balance of power and removes many situations liable to provoke hostilities. The policy of nonintervention, emphasizing national self-interest, provides a direction and purpose for our foreign policy, which is easily understood and readily accepted by the American people.

Peace is of the utmost importance, for it permits the preservation and expansion of individual liberty, where war does the opposite. A creative spirit requires it. This does not mean pacifism, for when our freedom and national security are directly threatened, defense is of the utmost importance and everyone should participate. Universal voluntary service in the defense of freedom is not an unreasonable expectation.

Carelessly entering into conflicts jeopardizes our liberty. It does not protect it. Intervention abroad causes us to neglect our obligations at home. The moral and constitutional obligations of our representatives in Washington are to protect our liberty, not coddle the world, precipitating no-win wars, while bringing bankruptcy and economic turmoil to our people. The people are demanding a change in foreign policy. Nonintervention is the policy that will serve us best.

Recognizing the nature of the enemy is critical. It is not weaponry or soldiers or politicians, but it is the ideology that is important. Robert Taft understood this clearly. He recommended:

> ...positive campaign in behalf of liberty. And when I say liberty I do not simply mean what is referred to as 'free enterprise'. I mean liberty of the individual to think his own thoughts and live his own life as he desires to think and to live; the liberty of the family to decide how they wish to live, what they want to eat for breakfast and for dinner and how they wish to spend their time; the liberty of a man to develop

> his ideas and to get other people to teach those ideas, if he can convince them that they have some value to the world.

It is our weakness in defense of liberty that presents the problem. A vacuum created by a philosophic complacency allows communist ideology to sweep into areas of the world whose only ideological defense comes through foreign aid funds confiscated from working Americans. This, in unaligned nations, provides no moral alternative to Communism, creates dependency by the receiving nations, and discourages those nations from defending themselves, while weakening ourselves economically, striking at the soul of our free system.

Without a firm belief in liberty, and an ability to present this belief clearly to the world in theory and in practice, victory is unlikely. Even a system doomed to failure—the U.S.S.R.—will persist insidiously, not from their strength but because of our weakness and ineptness.

Tragically the philosophy of collectivism pervades both East and West. It is this philosophy of state violence that prompts the building of weapons and the conscription of troops. It can be combated only with a philosophy of individual liberty based on natural rights.

We need to dispel the myths of collectivism that solidify power and privilege in the hands of the state, whether in Russia or in the United States. Then it would be unnecessary to compare dollars spent on the military, missiles, and gross national products of the two superpowers. Then the arms race would disappear.

Providing an adequate defense of our nation and our liberty is all that should concern us.

CHAPTER III

The Draft or Freedom

No one argues that the military draft is not an example of physical coercion, thus denying liberty to those drafted. But it is carelessly accepted by many, except those of draft age, as necessary to the preservation of a free society.

If one looks closely at the issue, one sees that conscription is a trait of totalitarian government, and is not characteristic of a nation that champions individual freedom. There are some who recognize that the draft is truly a violation of individual rights and oppose its imposition, except in extreme circumstances such as declared war. Even though a consistent defense of natural rights and individual freedom compels the rejection of the draft under all conditions, those who recognize their inconsistencies and would permit a draft only under emergency conditions are less of a threat to freedom than those who advocate peacetime conscription, with or without a national youth service.

It is this group, who either deliberately ignore or do not have the vaguest idea of what it means to live in a free society, that presents the greatest danger. For anyone developing a consistent political philosophy, the draft must be recognized as one of the most fundamental of all freedom issues.

Patriotism and the Draft

Patriotic Americans should courageously defend natural rights and individual freedom. Today's confusion has led many to believe that patriotism compels them to compromise on this one issue and to grant to the state the authority to draft our youth, against their wishes, to fulfill a carelessly devised, illogical and dangerously interventionist foreign policy.

For this reason we see many good conservative congressmen, with their patriotic ideals, championing the reinstitution of the draft. Patriotism should never be a justification for endorsing conscription. A patriotic American will instead guard against using the power of the state against the people under all circumstances.

It is in the American tradition to oppose a drafted military. For us, the drafted army is essentially a twentieth-century phenomenon. Its institution corresponds with the decline of our economic and personal freedoms and the rise of militarism. The drafted army dates roughly from the Wilson Administration and the First World War.

Although a draft was tried in the Civil War, it was met by stiff resistance and was never accepted, nor was it effective. It was so unpopular that it produced fewer than 50,000 soldiers, under 3 percent of the total forces. Some argue that it actually prolonged the war and did nothing to win it. Young men could avoid serving, even if drafted, by paying $300 to the government. This made the Civil War draft very different from what we have experienced in this century.

Patriotism should never be a justification for endorsing conscription.

The Founding Fathers never granted constitutional authority to the Congress or the President to conscript an army. The Ninth and Tenth Amendments are very clear in stating that if a power is not granted to the federal government, that power is "retained by the people." The argument that the constitutional authority "to raise and support armies" gives the federal government the authority to force a young man to serve in the military was explicitly rejected by the authors of the Constitution. In the Federalist Papers #41, James Madison wrote:

> It has been urged...that the power to lay and collect taxes ...to pay the debts, and provide for the defense and general

> welfare of the United States, amounts to an unlimited commission to exercise every power which may be alleged to be necessary for the common defense or general welfare. No stronger proof could be given of the distress under which these writers labor for objections than their stooping to such a misconception.

Certainly Madison believed that government authority must be explicitly granted. The argument that the common defense permits a draft is clearly a constitutional misconception.

Daniel Webster, a great champion of freedom and defender of the Constitution in his early Congressional years, was a staunch supporter of the voluntary military. In the War of 1812, there were many who wanted to impose the draft. Even as gunfire was heard near the Capital, Webster debated on the House floor and defeated the attempt to impose a draft for the "protection" of the country.

It should be remembered that without any draft in the War of 1812, as well as the Revolutionary War, our people fought and won with a sense of patriotism. Yet with the draft, with the millions of conscripted soldiers, with billions of dollars, and with all the advanced technology, we lost in Vietnam. Defending liberty and providing for an army is more complicated than merely imposing a draft on a select few.

Daniel Webster, in his great speech in the House in 1814, said:

> The question (of military conscription) is nothing less than whether the most essential rights of personal liberty be surrendered and despotism embraced in its worst form. . . Is this, sir, consistent with the character of a free government? Is this civil liberty? Is this real character of our Constitution? No, sir, indeed it is not. The Constitution is libeled, foully libeled. The people of this country have not established for themselves such a fabric of despotism. They have not purchased at a vast expense of their own treasure and their own blood a Magna Carta to be slaves. Where is it written in the Constitution, in what article or section is it contained, that you may take children from their parents, and parents from their children, and compel them to fight the battle in any war in which the folly or the wickedness of government may engage it? Who will show me any constitutional injunction which makes it the duty of the American? Who will show

> me any constitutional injunction which makes people surrender everything valuable in life, and even life itself, not when the safety of their country and its liberties may demand the sacrifice, but whenever the purposes of an ambitious and mischievous government may require it?

Finally in 1865, the states approved the Thirteenth Amendment which provides that "neither slavery nor involuntary servitude, except as punishment for a crime whereof the party shall have been duly convicted, shall exist within the United States." Denying that conscription is anything but involuntary servitude is a distortion of the clear language and intent of this amendment.

Nowhere do these statements indicate that Americans in the name of patriotism shall be forced to endorse conscription. Other great Americans have also taken a strong principled stand against a conscripted military. Robert A. Taft strongly opposed the draft, and he was never said to be "unpatriotic," even by his political opponents. In one of his great speeches on the subject, Senator Taft said:

> It is said that a compulsory draft is a democratic system. I deny that it has anything to do with democracy. It is far more typical of totalitarian nations than of democratic nations. It is absolutely opposed to the principles of individual liberty, which have always been considered a part of American democracy. Many people came to this country for the single purpose of avoiding requirements of military service in Europe. This country has always been opposed to a large standing army, and it has always opposed the use of the draft in times of peace. I shrink from the very setting up of thousands of draft boards, with clerks and employees and endless paper work and red tape, from the registration of 12 million men and the prying into every feature of their lives, their physical condition, their religious convictions, their financial status, and even hobbies.

Milton Friedman, the Nobel Prize-winning conservative economist said:

> We need a strong military. But strength depends on spirit and not merely numbers. Our military will be far stronger if we recruit it by methods consistent with the basic value

> of a free society than if we resort to the methods of a totalitarian society.

In the 1980 campaign for the Republican Presidential nomination, the two most conservative candidates opposed the draft. Their unchallenged patriotism never compelled them to endorse the draft or even peacetime registration. Congressman Phil Crane said on the House floor:

> The draft is a form of involuntary servitude which imposes unnecessary restrictions on the freedoms of draftees and their families alike...The American tradition is founded on an attachment to the principle of individual freedom. Imposition of a draft is contrary to that principle. It violates the spirit of the Thirteenth Amendment—protection against involuntary servitude.

In a speech at Louisiana State University in Baton Rouge, Louisiana, on September 23, 1980, Ronald Reagan spoke of his "vision of secure freedom" and his attitude to the draft:

> I oppose registration for the draft...because I believe the security of freedom can best be achieved by security through freedom. The all-voluntary force is based on the sound and historic American principle of voluntary commitment to defense of freedom...the United States of America believes a free people do not have to be coerced in defending their country or their values and that the principle of freedom is the best and only foundation upon which a defense of freedom can be made. My vision of a secure America is based on my belief that freedom calls forth the best in the human spirit and that the defense of freedom can and will best be made out of love of country, a love that needs no coercion. Out of such a love, a real security will develop, because in the final analysis, the free human heart and spirit are the best and most reliable defense.

These are great patriotic words, and it was this expression of love of country and the voluntary spirit that was responsible for the election of Ronald Reagan.

The war issue, used against conservative presidential candidates in the past, did not work in 1980, and Governor Reagan's position on the draft, in contrast to President Carter's, was largely responsible.

The American people know deep down that coercion is wrong and voluntarism is preferable. It certainly was a disappointment to see President Reagan change his mind regarding registration after the election. Unfortunately too many have been confused into believing that the patriotic position is to endorse the draft.

Another great patriotic American, Dan Smoot, said this about the draft in a letter to me:

> As I told you I was opposed to the draft even in 1950 when the Communist party and 'liberal' outfits that always followed the Communist line were the only others who opposed it. They opposed the draft because being statists they thought it would strengthen the United States to resist communism. I knew it would do just the opposite of that; yet, aware of the subtle difficulties of arguing against the draft on strictly constitutional grounds, I avoided those difficulties and built all my arguments on the unimpeachable assertion that a draft violates the spirit of liberty which brought Europeans here in the first place, and violates the principle of liberty which enables those transplanted Europeans to build a free society.

Judging from these quotes, it is clearly an error to assume that the conservative position is in support of the draft.

Conscription and Natural Rights

Conscription contradicts the whole concept of natural rights. If our lives and liberties are gifts of the Creator, as our Founding Fathers believed, the use of our lives should never be controlled by the State. If they are controlled, it supports the totalitarian notion that rights are mere privileges granted by the state and, therefore, removable at will by the state, an idea alien to the American tradition.

That is why it is so important that this most fundamental of all liberty issues—conscription—be thouroughly analyzed and understood.

There is a moral obligation for those living in a free country to participate in its defense; everyone of us has that obligation. This moral obligation, fulfilled voluntarily, cannot be confused with the suggested "morality" of someone owing a service to a government that demands a young man risk his life under threat of imprisonment.

Author John Hospers says: "The argument for the draft comes to this: 'I want you to protect me so badly that I'll gladly sacrifice your life so you can do this.' The answer is that my life is not yours to sacrifice."

Russell Kirk in the *Conservative Mind* states the argument against universal military training just as clearly:

> Universal military training, the most crushing burden that the state can impose upon its people...is found in conjunction with leveling democracy not merely by coincidence. The armed hoard is a concomitant of egalitarian socialism and state planning; and it is a natural reaction of any society which has abandoned all the old habitual and internal disciplines, so it must rely (as Burke predicted) upon arbitrary external discipline. Individuality, like imagination, must vanish from a people among whom socialism triumphs.

Not only will individuality vanish, but so too will individual liberty, as the resistance to compulsory military service disappears.

Ayn Rand said opposition to the draft is not to be confused with pacifism:

> Needless to say unilateral pacifism is merely an invitation to aggression. Just as an individual has the right of self-defense, so has a free country if attacked. But this does not give its government the right to draft men to military service, which is the most blatantly statist violation of a man's right to his own life.

The question boils down to this: can a free society be preserved by compromising on freedom itself? Or is the danger very real that once this compromise is made, the defense of all other freedoms becomes impossible? Although all freedoms of expression do not vanish overnight with the imposition of a draft, a blanket acceptance of conscription—especially in peacetime—will surely be followed by the demise of all other liberties as well.

Most conservatives reject compulsion in economic matters, yet accept the coercive role of government in forcing the innocent young to face battle. If conservatives permit the young to be forced to wear uniforms and risk their lives in undeclared wars like Korea and Vietnam, what intellectual defense is there against a similar grant of authority to the state to compel national civilian service? If a peace-time draft is acceptable to the American people, more arbitrary forms of people control will surely follow.

In the Second World War, Joseph Stalin made this very point. He was once asked by an American writer, according to Professor Dean Russell, how he (Stalin) could justify conscripting all the property of all the people for use by the government to fight the war. Stalin answered by asking why they considered it more immoral and illogical to conscript lifeless property than to conscript life itself, as was being done in the United States and all other capitalistic countries. His American challenger had no answer, because there was no answer.

Conservatives correctly reject registration of guns on constitutional and freedom grounds. They know that registration is merely a vehicle for later confiscation. It is disturbing to me that so many who see the importance of this liberty insist on registering their own sons with the government. Our young people's lives and liberty deserve at least as much consideration and constitutional protection as our guns.

If the liberty of our young people is neglected, the liberty required to maintain a free-market economy cannot be defended; the very foundation of liberty—the right to control our own lives—has been removed. An OSHA or EPA inspector can never be as much of a threat to our existence as an order directing us to the foxholes of a worthless foreign battlefield.

If the government can literally spend the lives of our youth in foolish military adventures, what argument is there against government's spending, controlling, and taxing away the fruits of our labors for less-dangerous things? There is none, and that is why statism, interventionism, socialism, and the loss of freedom in all areas of society have paralleled the gradual acceptance of a draft by the American people.

Unless we have a comprehensive defense of liberty which insists on economic and personal liberty, and correspondingly rejects compulsory service of all sorts, the consensus that a drafted army is proper will unfortunately prevail. Neither the conservative, who outlaws gambling and alcohol and homosexuality, nor the liberal, who regulates and taxes the economy, is likely to stand against the tide of those who desire to place an unfair military burden on our young people.

In conceding that conscription is a proper function of the State, one places the State above God, collective right above individual rights, planned economy above the market economy, and property above life itself. The patriotism, the devotion, the wisdom, the conviction, the commitment, and the idealism which we all seek and need for a free society to exist cannot be achieved by conscription. This tool, used by many states for centuries, has never built a free society, nor can it be used to preserve a free society.

Dean Russel in *The Conscription Idea* made this statement: "I have more faith in myself and in my fellow American than do the politicians and humanitarians who desire to defend my freedom by depriving me of it. "The strength of a free nation comes from the rightness of its policies and its people's convictions that the nation's purpose is noble and proper.

Freedom cannot be preserved by tyranny. Ultimately our decision on this most fundamental issue will tell us the direction in which our nation is going.

The Draft Is Unfair

Those who promote the draft actually believe it can be made to be fair. Even though they recognize the many shortcomings of previous drafts, they maintain vigorously that their plan for a draft will be fair. This is impossible.

There has *never* been a draft that was fair.

All attempts at making the draft equitable have used arbitrary and discriminatory power tactics that defy every precept of liberty. Conscripts are the ultimate victims of governmental rejection of our heritage and individual rights.

The inconsistency of supporting the draft while talking about "equal justice under the law," accepting that we have been "endowed by our Creator with certain inalienable rights, and among these are life and liberty" should be obvious to everyone.

Selective service is nothing more than deciding who shall die and who shall live. All the justification and rationalizations about fighting for noble causes cannot change this fact. When registration is initiated, the sentencing through government power of some young people to death begins. These are not murderous criminals, but innocent victims. How can anyone with a sense of morality participate in this crime against our children?

As Dean Russel stated:

> A mania for compulsory equality has swept this nation. It now applies to how we shall die or face death, as well as to how we shall work and be educated. It is as illogical in the one instance as it is in the other.

Not only is this mania illogical, economic equality or fairness in the draft is never achieved. Yet these egalitarian notions serve only to undermine our free society.

Even if we could distribute the death sentence without discrimination, it would still be a crime against God and man. Equal distribution of the risk of death and suffering is impossible. The attempts of some proponents of the draft to make it universal, both military and civilian, cannot correct these inequities.

Even the thought of universal conscription should chill the spine of any freedom-loving individual.

Bad wars cannot be fought without conscription. During the Korean War, only 17.7 percent of the armed forces were draftees, but 33.7 percent of those fighting in Vietnam were drafted.

The plain truth is that some will be sentenced to die and others will not. Nobody wants to think in these terms, but we have no choice.

How does one ration death? A government that believes it can ration gasoline equitably may be tempted to believe it can ration death as well.

Our gasoline allocation system led to gasoline lines; a conscription system will prompt lines leading to Canada, Europe, and Latin America. It is tragic to think that other countries can offer more freedom and security than America.

The problems which egalitarian conscriptors face are many:

Should only boys go, or girls as well?

> This question alone can rip America apart. Many religions teach that it is not the responsibility of women to bear arms, but to preserve and protect our homes. Soldiering, they believe, is a moral responsibility of men.

Are students exempt?

The feeling now is against the student exemption; however, given a shortage of MD's and other professionals and the arbitrary nature of conscription, those who promote the draft will surely reason that exemptions are, not only wise, but absolutely necessary. I can conceive of some student exemptions even being mandated.

Visual problems? Flat feet? Bedwetters? Homosexuality?

Why does one with a slight visual problem escape the death sentence? Flat feet used to save the young men from the rigors of foreign battle. What other silly medical exemption will preserve one life over another? Bedwetters were ruled exempt from conscription in the Second World War. Following this ruling, bedwetting promptly went up 1,200 percent in one Texas training camp. Those feigning homosexuality could also get an exemption.

Age?

This discrimination is the worst inequity of all. Why does the 45-year-old who has lived well and never served get off scot-free, staying home to reap the profits of military expenditures? How can anyone send an 18-year-old to death in a no-win foreign war and allow a war profiteer, who never served, to live in luxury?

Religion?

Religious exemptions have existed in the past, and will continue, I'm sure. Why is a Mennonite's refusal to fight honored, and a Baptist's met with a jail sentence? Are rights relative? If so, relative to what? They cannot be related if we believe in equal justice before the law.

It is obvious that we do not need to draft all of the 32 million people between the ages of 18 and 26. No matter how big a war erupts, the questions remains, which fraction will go and who shall choose? Selections must be arbitrary. The use of the Selective Service is the use of force and the threat of violence, methods that are unacceptable in a free society.

The obvious frustration of implementing a fair draft has led to the ultimate and so-called fair solution—the lottery. I cannot believe that conservatives who want to close the gambling houses would resort to gambling to choose who is to die and who is to live—and use this method in choosing who should be drafted.

Can we permit the lottery to be used to relieve politicians of their guilt for an arbitrary choice on who shall risk his life? Universal military service and the lottery are symbolic of the pro-draft people's desire to ration death sentences and escape the responsibility therein.

The use of the Selective Service is the use of force and the threat of violence, methods that are unacceptable in a free society.

Conscription must, of necessity, be selective and arbitrary. To argue otherwise defies logic. The selecting must be beneficial to one and deadly to another. Since conscription is the ultimate tax—the tax that takes a life and uses, maims, or even destroys it—its discriminatory distribution means we must reject the entire notion.

Amnesty for our recent draft dodgers established a fact: disobedience to draft laws preserves life, with punishment unlikely; obedience to draft laws means risk to one's life, with the rewards for service being society's scorn, possible physical injury, and perhaps even death. This recent history cannot be erased.

Just as many conservatives as liberals today have plans to protect their children by finding a safe haven for them if another "Vietnam" erupts. Of all the reasons why a draft cannot be fair and equitable, the amnesty exemption is the most repulsive to one who loves freedom and understands the need for a society guided by law and not ruled by men.

The states of marriage and of pregnancy raise many questions regarding the draft. Do the married have more right to live than the unmarried? According to most laws on conscription, they do. Justification for this defies logic and destroys the concept of equal rights. Marriage can be authentic or merely legal; many "paper-marriage contracts" have been drawn up in the past to escape the draft. If there were a marriage exemption, young people would flock ill-advisedly to the alter.

If married women were taken, could they be taken if pregnant? Should expectant mothers be treated differently from expectant fathers? Pregnancy in the first month is difficult to diagnose, so the cost of induction and discharge or providing care could be astronomical. How do you keep married women from getting pregnant? Or unmarried drafted women? Social acceptability of the unmarried mother, coupled with the advantage of escaping conscription, would provide a great incentive for getting pregnant. The heavy tax of conscription would prove a handsome subsidy to obstetricians.

Discrimination by numbers will occur, in spite of all the attempts to make the draft equitable. If 100,000 draftees are needed, or even 1,000,000, why must 32,000,000 register and become victims of civil rights discriminations?

Why must the noncommitted be subjected to exams, testing comparisons, and perhaps training, even if rejected for a good reason? The mere thought of instituting a really fair draft boggles the mind.

The risking of life in the defense of one's country must only be done with the consent of the individual. Otherwise life, freedom, liberty, natural rights, and equal protection under the law become only hollow words.

There is no philosophic defense for any part of freedom if we concede the right of the State to impose this maximum tax. The preservation of a society founded on the principle that rights come from God cannot be saved with a remedy based on state power over the individual.

The Draft and the Constitution

The Ninth Amendment to the Constitution states that just because certain rights have been listed in the Constitution, this "shall not be construed to deny" any others. And all these "others" are "retained" by the people—not a draft board brought into existence by an ill-advised Congress.

The Tenth Amendment is equally clear. Any power not specifically "delegated to the United States by Constitution" is "reserved to the state respectively or to the people."

These two amendments are the most frequently abused portions of our Constitution, since so little that is done in Washington these days is specifically authorized in the Constitution.

When I pointed this out one day to a colleague, with regards to the constitutionality of foreign aid, he became outraged and said, "The Constitution is not important," but "the laws we write, that permit us to appropriate the funds are." My suggestion that before these funds can be wasted overseas, they must first be stolen from the people made him livid and our conversation ended.

Both Madison and Webster argued against the draft from a constitutional viewpoint. They argued correctly that any action by the federal government must be authorized by the Constitution or the action is illegal. Conscription, its proponents argue, is authorized by Article 1, Section 8, Clauses 1, 12, 13, and 14: "Congress shall have power...to provide for the common defense and general welfare for the United States...to raise and support armies."

Neither Congress nor the President has the authority to draft or register anyone

---

Conscription is obviously not explicitly authorized by these or any other clauses, so its proponents fall back upon an implicit authorization. But conscription is not authorized by the Constitution, either explicitly or implicitly.

If conscription is not authorized by the Constitution, neither is registration, for registration has no purpose except as a means to execute conscription. Neither Congress nor the President has the authority to draft or register anyone.

The Hartford Convention in 1815, following the attempt to impose the draft in 1814, was adamant that there was no Constitutional authority to conscript. The convention reported:

> The effort to deduce this power from the right of raising armies is a flagrant attempt to pervert the Constitution. The armies of the United States have always been raised by contract, never by conscription, and nothing can be wanting in a government possessing the power thus claimed to usurp the entire control of the militia in derogation of the authority of the states, and to convert it by impressment into a standing army.

The convention also recommended a constitutional amendment against conscription, just as Rhode Island had insisted prior to being the last of the thirteen colonies to ratify the Constitution.

Robert Taft realized the significance of the error of accepting conscription as being constitutional and the danger of allowing force to be used to recruit individuals to serve in any capacity deemed important or necessary by the state.

With this type of mentality ruling Congress today, it is no wonder that the productive citizen now serves the nonproductive citizen as a fulfillment of the nonproducer's "rights." The goods and services that are provided to the nonproducers by wealth redistribution through taxation, inflation, or special economic regulations may be indirect as compared to conscription and national service, but the principle remains the same.

Taft in his 1940 speech clearly analyzed the illogical consequence of permitting a draft:

> The principle of a compulsory draft is basically wrong. If we must use compulsion to get an army, why not use compulsion to get men for other essential tasks? We must have men to manufacture munitions, implements of war, and war vessels. Why not draft labor for those occupations at wages lower than the standard? There are many other industries absolutely essential to defense, like the utilities, the railroads, the coal mining industries. Why not draft men for those industries, also at $21.00 a month? If we draft soldiers, why not draft policemen and firemen for city and state services? The logical advocates of the draft admit this necessary conclusion. Senator Pepper, of Florida has said that he believed the President should have power to draft men for munitions plants. Mr. Walter Lippman says that if the conscription bill is to serve its real purpose it must not be regarded as a mere device for putting one man out of twenty-five into uniforms, but must be regarded as a method of mobilizing the men of the country for much larger and more complicated task of industrial preparedness. In short, the logic behind the bill requires a complete regimentation of most labor and the assignment of jobs to every man available to work. This is actually done today in the communist and fascist state, which we are now apparently seeking to emulate.

Obviously, according to Taft, the draft is not constitutional.

The Court Rules

Two unfortunate Supreme Court decisions in 1918 and 1968 claimed the draft was constitutional. The fact that the Supreme Court has, on two occasions, ruled this way gives the conscriptor "credibility" and power, but it is hardly enough to make it morally correct and Constitutional. The Supreme Court has been in error before. Obviously a reversal of the opinions would be required if the draft is ever to be outlawed. These rulings permit the draft, but do not compel it—only Congress and the President can force the draft on our children.

And fortunately, we still do have something to say about who our representatives are and how they should act. The responsibility of interpreting the Constitution and imposing or not imposing the military draft still lies with the people through their representatives.

In the 1968 case, the United States vs. O'Brien, Earl Warren said that the power "to classify and conscript for military service is beyond question." This is the same Earl Warren who, as California Attorney General, helped inter Japanese-Americans in concentration camps and defended this action as being constitutional. Warren was notorious for ignoring the Constitution if it conflicted with his political prejudices.

For those who are pro-life, an analogy of the rights of the unborn to the rights of the teenage draftee are worth considering. If rights are universal, those two groups should be treated equally. The life of the unborn and the life of the 18-year-old should both receive equal protection under the law. The Supreme Court decision of 1973 said there was a relative value placed on *in-utero* life as being less valuable than *extra-utero* life.

A decade of struggle has not yet erased this inconsistency, but if we are to survive as a free and moral nation, this decision must also be reversed. Without its reversal, the relative value placed on life will lead to infanticide, euthanasia, and human experimentation. History has proven this, and consistent conservatives have supported this view. Relative value placed on human life by conscription is not unlike the examples above, which are arbitrary and discriminatory. Good conservatives fight for the right of even an unwanted, deformed, unborn child to live, yet at the same time seal this same child's fate through a lottery system that issues death sentences to be carried out on distant foreign soils for causes unknown.

The Civil War Challenge

During the Civil War, with Lincoln's assumption of war power, the issue of the draft never made it to the U.S. Supreme Court. Although, in a practical sense, the draft was a total failure for the Union, the fact that there was never a Supreme Court ruling against the draft meant the legal stage was set for the acceptance by the courts in 1918.

By then the growth of the collective mentality of the twentieth century permitted the general acceptance of compulsory military service. The cause of declining personal and economic freedoms since 1914 parallels the rise in popular support for compulsory military service—not surprisingly since they are one and the same.

There was one case of great importance in 1863, Kneedler vs. Lane, heard before the Pennsylvania Supreme Court, where the issue of conscription was considered in detail. The draft was ruled unconstitutional, only to be reversed by a new majority on the court two months later. The complainants based their case on the claim that the federal government had no power to compel military service, even in light of "insurrection," for the Constitution says that "repelling insurrection and repelling invasion will be a responsibility of the state militia," not the federal government.

In the majority opinion given at Pittsburgh, Pennsylvania, on November 9, 1863, which ruled the draft unconstitutional, the following comments were made by Chief Justice Lowrie:

> If Congress may institute (a draft law) as a necessary and proper mode of exercising its power 'to raise and support armies' then it...may compel people to lend it their money (or) take their houses...I am quite unable now to suppose that so great a power could have been intended to be granted, and yet be left so loosely guarded.

Two other Justices, Woodward and Thompson, agreed with Chief Justice Lowrie by adding:

...assuredly the framers of our Constitution did not intend to subject the people of the states to a system of conscription which has applied in the mother country only to paupers and vagabonds...Times of rebellion, above all others, are the times when we should stick to our fundamental law, lest we drift into anarchy on one hand, or into despotism on the other. The great sin of the (present) rebellion consists in violating the Constitution, whereby every man's civil rights are exposed to sacrifice...the argument is that the exigencies of the times justify the substitution of martial law for the constitution.

And Justice Thompson further added:

> We cannot suppose that at the moment the country had achieved its liberty...that such a despotism over the lives and liberties of men, would be incorporated into the Constitution as conscription. As if by the agency of the pressgang. . . the Constitution was adopted in ignorance, certainly, of any such power, if it does exist, it has required the lapse of three-quarters of a century to develop its latent evils. The moral evidences are all against the idea (of the draft).

Two months later Chief Justice Lowrie's term expired, and the opinion was reversed by a court order vacating the injunction against the draft, in itself an unconstitutional maneuver. The only proper means by which a ruling like this could be overruled would be for a higher court to do so, and in this case it would have had to be the U.S. Supreme Court. No new facts were entered, no new affidavits were entered; the injunction was merely vacated.

J. L. Bernstein, who wrote up this case in the *American Bar Association Journal* in 1967, said:

> In my reading of law, I have never come across a more fascinating opinion than Kneedler...It was obvious that the government had no desire for a full-dress review in the court of last resort, despite President Lincoln's (publicly) expressed hope for it.''

That forthcoming ruling was not to appear until 1918, following the imposition of the draft in the First World War. Without the chance of the Pennsylvania case going to the Supreme Court, the squelching of the real constitutional dissent for the draft set the stage for the first disastrous U.S. Supreme Court ruling on the draft in 1918. In dealing with the issue of the Thirteenth Amendment, it was clear that the justices in 1918 believed in the constitutionality of the draft only in a declared war. The need for a draft should come only ''as a result of war declared by the great representative body of the people."

The Court was hardly thinking about our adventures in Korea and Vietnam as qualifying. Since they did not comment, we will be fighting undeclared wars. Justice Douglas in his dissent on May 20, 1968, in a similar case contested this precise point—that if a draft is constitutional, it is definitely limited only to times of declared war by the Congress, and should not apply to careless police actions engaged by an ill-advised Administration:

> This is undoubtedly true (the right to conscript) in times when by declaration of Congress, the nation is in a state of war. The underlying and basic problem in this case, however, is whether conscription is permissible in the absence of a declaration of war. That question has not been briefed nor was it presented in oral argument, but it is, I submit, a question upon which the litigants and the country are entitled to a ruling.

Justice Douglas is absolutely correct on this point. But I believe the American people are entitled to a complete hearing on the entire point of constitutionality—with the viewpoint expressed that would defend individual liberty more consistently, getting a better hearing than we have had in these past two Supreme Court rulings. A ruling limiting the draft to declared war only would be beneficial, although far from perfect.

Current court opinion claiming the constitutionality of conscription should not sway our opinion, since we know the history of this decision, as well as other decisions of the Supreme Court.

The Congress is given the primary responsibility—one they have flagrantly ignored—for interpreting the Constitution. The people, with their voice in Washington, can reverse the trend of freedom erosion whenever they put their mind to it. Then the oath taken by each Representative to uphold the Constitution will mean something.

The Draft: the Final Blow

Military dictatorships are usually built on brute force, but on occasion one is built on deliberate court and legislative actions. The attitude expressed by the Supreme Court as it declared a male-only draft constitutional, opens the door to abuse by the military and encourages the conditions that are destined to drive us to war.

A constitutional crisis has been ongoing in this country for decades.

On opinions regarding busing, bilingual education, hiring procedures, prison reform, taxes and abortion, the courts have ignored the Constitution and rewritten laws to impose social reforms of their choosing.

This attitude could not have been more evident than in the Supreme Court ruling that permits registration of some men (18-21-year-olds) and no women. This ruling, Rostker (Director of the Selective Service) vs. Goldberg 1981, dramatizes this crisis and demonstrates to what depths we have fallen.

It is apparent that the official regard for the Constitution, for individual liberty and constitutional principle, is so calloused as to prompt great disenchantment with the judicial system. The Court held on June 25, 1981:

> The act's registration provisions do not violate the Fifth Amendment. Congress acted well within its constitutional authority to raise and regulate armies and navies when it authorized the recognition of men and not women.

The conclusion, therefore, is that rights are relative, allowing some citizens to be victimized more easily than others. If the "due process" clause of the Fifth Amendment affords no protection, why doesn't the Ninth, or Tenth, or the Thirteenth?

This question was not even addressed by the Court. Even the equality they refuse to protect was an aberrant version. The desire of some women for "equality" by demanding equal injury with men by being drafted was hardly an appropriate way to demand equal justice before the law. Nevertheless, the Court was deliberate in ignoring the issue of equal justice.

Assuming that any function of government can be accomplished by conscripted labor is a dangerous and untenable assumption in a free society. Authority "to raise an army" cannot be construed as power to force service while ignoring the Ninth, Tenth, and Thirteenth Amendments.

If this is the case, power to conscript Supreme Court Judges at $10 per week, civil service workers to deliver the mail, or workers in plants providing weapons for military use would then be acceptable. This possibility cannot be ignored and remains a true danger as one studies exactly what the Court said in Rostker vs. Goldberg.

At the rate we are going, it is not impossible to assume someone will eventually include these other functions of government as well. The mere fact that the Constitution authorizes certain precise responsibilities to government is no justification for the use of force to conscript people to perform those functions or services. The exact opposite is the case.

This one assumption can serve as the ultimate tear, never to be repaired again, in the document meant to preserve our liberty from men determined to rule over other men. The story of history is the story of men seeking control over others, ignoring the desire of most who demand and expect that their lives be their own, uncontrolled by others. This ruling further confirms my concern that personal liberty is on the wane and constitutional protection of all our liberties is threatened.

If ever there was an area needing constitutional restraints placed upon an Administration or Congress, it is in the area of ''military affairs.''

The mere fact that the Constitution authorizes certain precise responsibilities to government is no justification for the use of force to conscript people to perform those functions or services

---

All areas of concern should be treated exactly equal; however, a constitutional responsibility of the courts should be exactly the same regardless of the issue at hand. Yet the Court assumes a relative responsibility (Rostker vs. Goldberg):

> The customary deference accorded Congress's judgments is particularly appropriate when, as here, Congress specifically considers the question of the acts' constitutionality, and perhaps in no other area has the Court accorded Congress greater deference than in the area of national defense and military affairs.

Great deference in ''military affairs'' is not what is needed to prevent war. This ''great deference'' in the twentieth century for military affairs has brought us four major wars and hundreds of thousands of deaths and injuries.

The Court further confirmed this rejection of responsibility by saying they were anxious to: "dispel any concern that we (the Court) are injecting ourselves in an inappropriate manner in military affairs."

The Court describes a horrible attitude toward war preparation:

> Congress's determination that any future draft would be characterized by a need for combat troops was sufficiently supported by testimony adduced at the hearings so that the courts are not free to make their own judgment on the question.

"Need for troops" is all that's required as determined by Congress, and to the Court the purpose of the troops was unimportant as was the concept of individual liberty.

The Court further stated that: "Congress was entitled in the exercise of its constitutional powers to focus on the question of military needs rather than 'equity'." The thought that "military needs" is deserving of greater protection than "equity" and justice before the law is a staggering thought and the fertile ground on which military dictatorship can flourish.

In other words, there are no restraints on Congress as long as what is done is in the name of "military need." That fact should frighten any decent, peace-loving American.

The Court, to describe its indifference to addressing the rights question involved, both to individuals facing the draft and to women being treated differently from men, used words like "strict scrutiny" being replaced by "minimum scrutiny."

Minimum it was; a rights concern it was not! This deference to Congress in military affairs is done by applying the "important government interest" test. In other words, "government interests" are superior to "individual rights."

I have sensed this for years, but to read this in a Supreme Court ruling is nevertheless frightening and exasperating. To our Supreme Court, important government interests are superior concerns to important individual rights of life and liberty.

The Court in Rostker vs. Goldberg admitted that there was no "area of governmental activity in which courts have been less competent" than in military matters. In this case a lot more was involved than a military opinion on training, a most basic question of protecting individual liberty. To that qualification, I agree; the courts are "incompetent."

Their main concern and argument was that Congress had previously written legislation prohibiting women from engaging in combat and were justified in doing so. Therefore, it was impractical to register women. The military argued that those behind the lines may be pulled up in emergencies; if women were involved, they could not be brought to the front lines. In essence, the law and military needs supercede the constitutional protection of individual rights.

If a voluntary military were to exist, and the military were to exist for the defense of one's homeland, no prohibition against women engaging in combat would be necessary. Women are capable of defending their families and homes and country, and outright prohibition against even their voluntary participation in combat should be an insult to all of us.

Recently, a woman who had just witnessed her husband being shot by two burglars was forced to a decision as they held a gun to her son's head. Calling upon her recent pistol training for such an occasion, she pulled out two pistols and shot and killed both intruders.

Defense in combat, done voluntarily and for actual defensive purposes, is the responsibility of all citizens of a free country. Prohibition against some participants in combat and compelling others against their wishes to participate in worldwide military adventurism (sanctioned by the Court) is a significant reason for sorrow for those who love freedom and the Constitution.

The Court claims that the Constitution grants "explicit" authority to draft men by the clause in the Constitution permitting Congress to "raise" an army. This should not even be implicit, since all authority not given specifically is denied by the Ninth and Tenth Amendments. Raise an army? Yes. Conscript an army? No!

If a voluntary military were to exist, and the military were to exist for the defense of one's homeland, no prohibition against women engaging in combat would be necessary

---

The argument that the Court should not concern itself with individual rights and thus grant "deference" to the Congress on military matters is unbelievably shallow. The Court claims they should not interfere in matters of the military—i.e., the draft, discipline in the military, who shall serve, etc.—because they (the Court) don't want the military "intervening in judicial matters."

The Supreme Court put great weight on the Senate report which claimed that rapid mobilization of troops for combat was "essential to the preservation of our national security." And, "a functioning registration system is a vital part of any mobilization plan."

Yet the plain truth is that rapid deployment of American youngsters (unanxious to enter battle) to troubled spots throughout the world in a quick decision by a nervous Defense Secretary in the middle of the night is a threat to our national security. It is not something that would enhance it.

Rapid deployment of troops and accelerated call-ups of young men, even without a declaration of war, should not be encouraged by our top court. Deployment should be dealt with in a constitutional and deliberate manner, for the issue is of a profound nature and has most serious consequences.

Let there be no doubt as to the courts' interpretation of Congress' intention in requiring registration: "The purpose of registration, therefore, was to prepare for a draft of *combat* troops" (their emphasis). Since women are not permitted in combat by law, they are thus rejected from registration.

A lower court, in ruling that social security numbers cannot be required at the time of registration, stated: (U.S. District Court, District of Columbia, November 24, 1980) "Citizens have a duty to serve in the Armed Forces and a correlative right to register unimpeded by an invasion of their privacy unless statutorily authorized."

This remarkable sentence tells us of the gobbledy-gook coming out of our courts. Those required to register deserve "privacy" and should not be required to provide their social security numbers, yet no concern whatsoever was shown for an individual's "privacy" being protected from being sent by force to some battlefield to face death or crippling in a no-win undeclared war.

The remarkably shallow understanding and callous disregard for individual rights seen in this ruling is demonstrated by the suggestion that even this pittance of privacy afforded by the Privacy Act needs only be eliminated by a crass piece of congressional legislation—which they subsequently passed in July 1981.

They couldn't care less about the *real* privacy protection afforded by the U.S. Constitution!

In ruling against women being required to register, the Court uses the Senate report's statement that this view "is universally supported by military leaders" ignoring the basic issue of individual rights. If a violation of individual rights can be justified because "military leaders support it" and the real issue ignored because of the demands of the military leaders, woe be unto us—for our whole judicial system then is threatened.

The ruling was principally defended by quoting from the Senate report as if it were the supreme law of the land. The Constitutional questions of forced servitude and individual rights were totally ignored. Their attitude was that if Congress ignored the Constitution in their deliberations on the draft, and felt registration and the draft necessary for military needs, then they, the Court, need not concern themselves either.

The two dissenting views offered no hope. These views merely argued for the rights of some to be victimized equally as men, for the sake of military matters. No principled argument was presented to demand equal protection of the law by insisting neither men nor women be forced to serve against their wishes.

The low regard for constitutionally protected individual rights as expressed in this Supreme Court ruling is disconcerting and is further evidence that the direction in which this country is going is discouraging and dangerous. The fact that the courts now have reneged on their responsibility for evaluating what Congress is doing with regards to conscripting a small segment of the population to serve another larger segment, is essentially sanctioning any authority the Congress wants in preparation for and entering into war.

Economic conditions as they are and military preparations going on—in spite of the fact that we are not at this particular time in conflict—are indicative that there are strong forces determined to lead us unwisely into armed conflict.

For the first time in our history, we significantly increased the military budget 70 percent to be used to defend nations other than America, even though we are not in a war. This, along with the Supreme Court's sanctioning the drafting of men for the purpose of combat, is certainly a sign that we are closer to war than we have been in many years.

The Draft and Economics

Not only is the draft ill-advised for patriotic, moral, and constitutional reasons, it is harmful for economic reasons as well. The draft is a form of tax—a very unfair one at that—and is economically inefficient. Many supporters of conscription sincerely believe we could not afford to pay for the services we need. But in the reality of this modern age, we cannot afford to allow low-paid, unhappy conscripts to work with the high technology required to defend America.

The draft is a form of tax—a very unfair one at that—and is economically inefficient.

If we are looking for ground troops for some ill-advised unnecessary armed conflict, possibly a role for an 18-year-old toting a rifle can be found. Even then it's doubtful, since the cost/benefit calculations do not justify it. We need highly skilled technicians today and decent pay is essential.

I've never heard suggestions that crucial jobs such as a jet pilots or ship captains be filled by draftees. Skilled jobs in the Navy, Air Force, and Marines have always been filled by volunteers for a specific reason—efficiency.

The late Admiral Ben Moreel, whose Seabees set such a magnificent example during World War II, refused ever to accept draftees. His reason for this was that the draft was not only an intrusion of the individual's freedoms, but it was also militarily inefficient.

Training draftees and preparing them for battle is very inefficient and expensive; time and money is always wasted. Defenders of the draft are quick to point out that defense manpower costs increased from $22 billion in 1964 to $50 billion in 1976.

But in 1977, a Rand Corporation study showed that virtually none of this increase could be attributed to the all-voluntary-force: "The end result is that the voluntary force has added less than $300 million to the cost of defense manpower, a fraction of the defense budget." Even this would not be necessary if the numbers were adjusted to needs and commitments throughout the world were changed.

Nobody has proven that large numbers of troops with rifles are superior to highly paid volunteers trained in modern technology for the defense of our country.

Today the United States is the most highly industrialized nation in the world. It has the largest accumulation of capital and its economy is the most efficient on earth, despite the current meddling by government planners.

We cannot hope to match the manpower of the Soviet Union or Communist China. It would be madness to send American men or women to fight the masses that the world's dictatorships can mobilize with nothing more advanced than a rifle and a bayonet.

Our armed forces should be capital-intensive, not labor-intensive, just like our agriculture. The masses of China cannot out-produce our farmers. The same is true in the military. A strong national defense can be achieved with a smaller, well-paid, highly trained defense force dedicated to making peace and avoiding war. The military needs to be equipped with the most sophisticated weapons that our scientists can develop. Masses of manpower provided by a draft would be useless to this type of military, and would actually be harmful.

Dean Russell emphasized the economic advantage of a voluntary army by comparing it to slavery.

> Actually, as any student of human action and motivation in a free market can understand, the slave owners could have made more money by freeing their slaves and paying them wages. For the same reason, conscripts and conscription are less effective and less efficient than volunteers and voluntary action...the average conscript will always cost more to do less than the average volunteer.

In the scramble to reinstate the draft, it is rarely pointed out that the great shortage is with experienced men who, out of frustration with morale and pay, are getting out of the service. The draftee won't help solve this problem. A Brookings Institute study in June 1979 said $300 million could be saved by retaining older personnel and decreasing the number of new recruits.

The wages of the first-termers have decreased by 15 percent, as compared to civilian employees in the three years prior to 1982. When this is compared to civilian government employees, the relative decrease is even more. It is natural to see less interest when real pay decreases. It is an utter disgrace to see our military personnel qualify for food stamps.

Milton Friedman has pointed out that the draft is nothing more than a vicious and unfair tax. Economist William Meckling agrees:

> Once we understand that conscription is a tax, it is easy to see why Congressmen find it appealing, especially at a time when they are under a great popular pressure to reduce taxes.

> Reinstitution of a specialized hidden tax will enable them to preserve a larger government than would be possible if they were forced to rely entirely on explicit general taxes.

This is particularly appealing to the average conservative who is anxious to keep up the military and cut taxes. This gets them off the hook and takes a little bit of pressure off cutting well-guarded domestic programs.

The true cost to society of a drafted army is never apparent to us. The concept of hiring cheap labor and saving dollars can be seen as a tax on those drafted, causing them to pay an unfair share of the defense bill. The total cost to society is a little more difficult to see and cannot be measured.

If an engineer is conscripted to peel potatoes, society loses the economic contribution of an engineer and gains a potato peeler. If the engineer generates $60,000 worth of productive effort, and the potato peeler $10,000 of productive effort, the net productive effort has been reduced by 84 percent. The true measurement of economic loss is not a comparison to the fair wage to do the job in the military, but the wage (productive effort) which that person would have earned or performed had he not been drafted.

Professor Friedman, in claiming the draft is the most vicious and unfair tax which any government can place on a particular group, says that it is also unnecessary and inefficient. It is the opposite of the graduated income tax. With the income tax, the more you earn the more you pay at a higher percent.

But an 18-year-old is supposed to owe a debt to the government and must pay this heavy tax to provide freedom for the 40-50-year olds who may never have served. It is more of a transfer payment from the poor defenseless young to the middleaged wealthy, protected by the congressmen, who believe this form of taxation is an example of American patriotism and absolutely necessary. Why does a businessman or a congressman who has reaped many blessings from our country owe less than the 18-year-old?

In today's world of advanced technology, don't the middleaged have a lot more to contribute to the military than the young? The answer given me when I ask this is that disrupting a man's life in the middle of his career is annoying and inconvenient. Don't they consider the "annoyance" and inconvenience to the 19-20-year-old who has his education, his marriage, his fatherhood, his career canceled by the government so that he can go to Korea or Vietnam to suffer loss of limb or life?

Basil Liddel Hart, the distinguished British military historian, came to his "present conviction of the supreme importance of freedom through the pursuit of efficiency" and for this reason after 25 years of study:

> ...changed my earlier and conventional belief in the value of conscription. It brought me to see that the compulsory principle was fundamentally inefficient and the conscription method out of date—a method that clung like the ivy, to quantitative standards in an age when the trend of warfare was becoming increasingly qualitative. For it sustained the fetish of mere numbers at a time when skill and enthusiasm were becoming ever more necessary for the effective handling of the new weapons. Conscription does not fit the conditions of modern warfare.

The claim made by many government draft proponents and especially those advocating universal service, is that it is good and necessary

---

But an 18-year-old is supposed to owe a debt to the government and must pay this heavy tax to provide freedom for the 40-50-year-olds who may never have served.

---

discipline. If parents fail in their responsibilities, they reason, the army can fulfill the role of disciplinarian and builder of character. Russel Kirk in his article *Conscription Ad Infinitum* (1946) demolishes this idea as impractical and mere wishful thinking.

> Abstract humanitarianism has come to regard servitude—as long as it be to the state—as a privilege. Greater self-love has no government than this: that all men must wear khaki so that some men may be taught to brush their teeth. Apologists for Negro slavery claimed for their peculiar institution the virtue which humanitarians now ascribe to the draft: that it instills healthful discipline.

I cannot imagine anything more preposterous than the "efficiency experts'' at the Pentagon (or any part of government) being responsible and expected to teach discipline to supposedly ''free'' individuals. The two are incompatible. This notion of the state disciplining youth prompts the ''training'' and conditioning of youths in all fascists and communist societies. For a nation to remain free, the role of the State must certainly never be seen as that of ''disciplinarian'' or as that of a ''builder of character.''

Efficiency of the Draft

If one cannot oppose the draft for the moral, economic, constitutional, and patriotic reasons already given, it should be rejected for military reasons alone. Since the declared purpose of the draft is to provide for a strong military, and since it does not achieve that, there is no purpose in it. It is assumed by most that war could not be fought without a draft. This may be true for offensive unpopular wars, but not for defensive warfare.

How effective would you be if your neighbor forced you into his service, to go with him to procure cattle from another neighbor, with weapons to kill if anyone interfered?

Compare this to defending your family from an armed hoodlum who bursts into your home to steal and threatens the lives of your family. In the defensive situation, it would be much easier to shoot to kill.

Although done with noble intentions, Korea and Vietnam can hardly be compared to defending your family from an armed aggressor. There is good evidence to show that, in these careless wars, most conscripted soldiers never shoot to kill.

A conscripted army is more likely to precipitate, expand, and prolong a war. Senator Robert Taft in a lesser-known ''Gettysburg Address'' given by him on May 30, 1945, at Gettysburg Cemetery, agreed that a drafted army was much more likely to lead to war than to peace:

> Military conscription is essentially totalitarian. It has been established for the most part in totalitarian countries and their dictators led by Napoleon and Bismarck. It has heretofore been established by aggressor countries. It is said it would insure peace by emphasizing the tremendous military protection of this country. Surely we have emphasized that enough in this war. No one can doubt it. On the contrary, if we establish

> conscription every other nation in the world would feel obliged to do the same. It would set up militarism on a huge pedestal throughout the world as the goal of all the world. Militarism has always led to war and not peace.

Some outstanding historians present a good case for a stalemated, early settlement of World War I had we not entered into it with a *holy* cause to make the world safe for democracy. Without the First World War, the peace settlement that helped precipitate the Second World War would not have been drawn up.

A conscripted army is more likely to precipitate, expand, and prolong a war.

In totalitarian societies, conscripted armies are the norm and are "useful" at times, but only when the spirit of freedom lies dormant.

Since the spirit of freedom never completely dies, even the military cannot be trusted when civil strife erupts, as the South American dictators have experienced for decades. When a dictatorial system suppresses individual liberty and economic liberty on a daily basis, rebellion among the ranks may be held in check for a time, and the people can be forced to fight aggressive, offensive wars.

Today Russia can still use her people to fight in Afghanistan, but the troops of Poland cannot be trusted to toe the line and suppress their own people when their real desire is to maximize their own personal freedom. The free Polish spirit could burst the bonds of oppression, and both the Polish and Russian communist dictators know it.

Americans would never have fought in Vietnam had our love of freedom not suffered the erosion during this century, for there would not have been a conscripted army to draw upon.

In a free society, patriotism and love of one's country serve to bring out the very best in its citizens—just as we would all struggle to the death if we saw our families being threatened by a murderer—when the nation is in jeopardy and needs to be defended. Under these conditions, force would add nothing but confusion.

In a free nation, if force—in the form of a draft—is necessary, the war is wrong or the spirit of freedom is too weak. Rarely does anyone fail to respond to an attack as a natural reflex in the defense of their person, their family, or their country. Aggressive intervention is unnatural. Most participants have to be taught job psychology or literally forced to kill. In defensive war, killing (if necessary) is a mere reflex and need not be taught.

The draft is never a sign of strength unless the nation is not free and offensive war is planned. In the congressional debates of 1979-1980 for the reinstitution of registration for the draft, the main argument of the proponents was that it was to be "a sign of strength," a "symbol" to Russia to persuade them to forgo any future aggression. This was prompted by the invasion of Afghanistan by Russia, and was to be our answer to communist expansion and threat of expansion around the world. Dictatorial communism was to be stopped by diminishing basic freedoms in America—an absurd notion.

Claiming that the draft or the threat of a draft with registration is a sign of strength, while continuing to finance the enemy through unwise foreign aid and loans through the Export-Import Bank, Commodity Credit Corporation, and other International Development banks, is self destructive on the part of America.

We paid for the road to Afghanistan, built by the American Corps of Engineers, and subsidized the Russian truck plant that built the trucks that hauled the troops through a subsidy from the Export-Import Bank. After getting concerned about the threat of Russian invasion into Poland, we quickly sent millions in loans to solidify the power of the communist dictators.

Instead of eliminating all of these subsidies to our enemies, we respond by delivering up our children.

In the last ten years, the Communist block has borrowed over $90 billion from the West, and the borrowing continues at the American taxpayers' expense, indirectly through the international banking institutions such as the International Monetary Fund, by protecting all banks who loan money through various government regulations.

These self-destructive acts cannot be canceled out by this show of strength, the draft. The registration/draft, especially under these conditions is a sign of weakness, not strength, and confirms our intention of self-destruction.

The concept of voluntarism in raising an army guards against unwise military involvements and thus acts to prevent war. Our Constitution was written to make sure a President could not enter into war without a declaration from Congress. Even if this were done and not endorsed by the people, the people would have another vote. Their lack of support would prevent the pursuance of war. The people could refuse to loan the funds to the government and could refuse to join the military if, in their opinion, it was unwise.

We should *insist* on these restraints provided by the Constitution to prohibit a war from occurring without the consent of the Congress and the people, and *insist* on a voluntary military and legitimate means to finance the war. Then those who would get us carelessly involved in war could not do so.

Today there are minimal restraints on military adventurism. Both Korea and Vietnam were fought without declaration, financed by congressionally created inflation, not legitimate taxation or borrowing, and fought with a conscripted military. The constitutional protection against careless war has been entirely removed. The ultimate protection against careless war in a free society is prohibition against the draft, allowing the citizens a choice about serving.

The constitutional protection against careless war has been entirely removed.

If conscription is good for privates on the front line, why don't we conscript generals from the corporate world?

Brigadier General S.L.A. Marshall in analyzing World War II, agrees with Liddell Hart. He claims that after deep study he found between 12-25 percent of those expecting to fire weapons actually did all the shooting required to win the war. He described one episode on Makin Island, overrun by the Japanese, in which only 37 out of over 1,000 American soldiers fired their weapons. In another battle on Chance Island, out of the 100-plus well-trained riflemen trapped, only 14 did the firing. General Marshall reports the record was even worse in Korea.

James Martin in his excellent article "A Look At Conscription Then and Now," quotes from *Colliers* magazine:

> In an attempt to increase the percent of those firing their weapons, psychiatrists were called in for recommendations. The report said: 'The most efficient method is to prompt them to lose their individual identities by prompting mob psychology for the purpose of breaking down inhibitions against killing.'

As a physician myself, I find this professional medical advice repugnant. Having been trained to preserve life and help bring new life into the world, reading physicians descriptions of how to condition men to kill against their nature is atrocious—especially since it's only in offensive or unnecessary war where killing is not a matter of reflex (as it is when we are truly defending our family or our country).

Dan Smoot took a principled, consistent stand against the draft for the benefit of an efficient national defense:

> If we concentrated on the kind of homeland defense we need, it could be manned by a relatively small group of professionals who could be hired in the open market for salaries attractive enough to compete with those offered by private industry and who could be given the intensive, extensive training necessary for their duties.

Many people make their decisions for or against the draft for different reasons: moral, constitutional, military, or economic. Ayn Rand claimed, "There is no contradiction between the moral and the practical: a volunteer army is the most efficient army, as many military authorities have testified."

A free country has never lacked volunteers when attacked by a foreign aggressor, but not many men would volunteer for such ventures as Korea and Vietnam. Without drafted armies, a foreign policy of military adventurism would not be possible.

A great Congressman, Howard Buffett, on the House floor in 1951, predicted that the acceptance of the draft idea would lead to the downfall of America as a great nation, and supported his contention with a review of 150 years of world history. Where American and Great Britain grew with classical liberalism and rejection of the draft idea, the twentieth century has shown a decline of both nations as they endorse conscription, a result of a less vigorous defense of individual liberty. Buffet stated:

> Universal military training brought defeats and disaster to France, Germany, Italy, and Japan. In none of these nations were the civilian components then able to maintain the necessary supremacy over the military...what sound reason can anyone give to support the claim that the fatal germs contained in peace time conscription elsewhere will not develop here?

He concluded by saying that universal military training will not prevent war and will not assure victory in case of war. Certainly the entry into defeat that we experienced in Vietnam bears out his prediction. Let us hope we can act to prevent the disaster which faces us unless we change our ways.

Milton Friedman said that over the years he has come into contact with many persons concerned with the draft, those who favor it and those who oppose it. He has seen many who initially favored the draft change their minds after studying the issue, but he has "never observed anyone who was initially in favor of a voluntary force reverse his position on the basis of further study."

At one time I endorsed the draft as a "necessary evil" to preserve freedom, but on further study of this issue, I have reversed my position. As my ideas of freedom have matured, my hostility and disdain for compulsion (as so clearly practiced in conscription) has grown. I have concluded that the draft, as a legitimate function of the state, can never be justified.

CHAPTER IV

Sound Money is Gold

The most significant political event of the twentieth century has been the loss of the concept of individual rights in the United States.

It is now commonplace to totally ignore what the Constitution says about individual rights while concentrating on a distorted interpretation of the general-welfare clause that prompts thousands of laws mandating economic equality, quota systems, hiring practices, pay scales, insurance rules, and a lot of other nonsense. (Chapter 1)

Running a close second in harm done has been our interventionist foreign policy pursued throughout most of this century. It's this policy of meddling overseas and entering carelessly into "entangling alliances," against which George Washington so rightly warned, that has caused so many unnecessary military casualties and greatly jeopardized America's security. (Chapter 2)

The most important economic event in this century has been the rejection of the gold standard, along with the establishment of a powerful central bank. The United States has led the world to the brink of financial collapse by ignoring the Founding Fathers' directive to avoid paper money. The establishment of the Federal Reserve System, our central bank, in 1913, and subsequent deliberate elimination of the gold standard, has permitted the accumulation of debt around the world on a scale never known in the history of man.

The irredeemable dollar, used as the reserve currency of the world since 1945, has allowed all nations of the world to live with inflation and deficits of gigantic proportions. Although the size of today's problem is overwhelming, the seeds of destruction were planted early in this century when the special interests, who are served by paper money, established the Federal Reserve System.

America is destined to pay a price for our extravagant living through a depression of gigantic proportions. The issues of individual rights, foreign policy, and monetary policy are not separate entities. When the crisis hits, we will be forced to reassess all our values and once again restate them as the Founding Fathers did 200 years ago. Careful study and understanding of monetary policy is crucial if we hope to effect positive changes during the next decade.

The Constitution and Money

The Constitution allows for a silver or gold standard, prohibits paper money, and does not authorize a central bank. Congress is explicitly given power to coin money in Article I, Section A, but no similar power was given to print fiat money.

The low respect for constitutionally guaranteed individual rights is precisely the same reason we as a nation have totally ignored the admonitions and directives of the Founding Fathers regarding money.

The debates at the Constitutional Convention clearly indicate a rejection of the proposal to "emit bills of credit" (irredeemable paper money). Even without the Convention's specific vote rejecting paper money, a specific authorization is required if paper money is to be issued, since the Tenth Amendment prevents Congress from assuming power to create money and credit out of thin air as it does today.

In Article I, Section 10, the Constitution explicitly prohibits states from emitting bills of credit and directs all states to use only gold and silver coins as legal tender in the payment of debts.

The low respect for constitutionally guaranteed individual rights is precisely the same reason we as a nation have totally ignored the admonitions and directives of the Founding Fathers regarding money.

The Founding Fathers were well-informed and were recovering from a currency crisis with the continental dollar when they met in Philadelphia to draft the Constitution. "Not worth a continental" was an ongoing reality for all of the attendees. Interstate trade barriers and runaway inflation with the continental dollar were the two main reasons the convention was convened. Some today would distort the intention of the framers of the Constitution with regard to money, but that is only to serve the interests of those who benefit from inflation.

It is interesting and important that, within the same sentence that Congress is given the power to coin money, it is also given the power to fix the standard of weights and measures. Clearly it was intended that the monetary unit be fixed in a precise weight of gold or silver. The phrase to "regulate the value thereof" has been grossly misinterpreted in the twentieth century.

Our leaders and courts have chosen to misinterpret this phrase to regulate the value of paper money by perpetual inflation—a mockery of the Founder's intentions. The phrase permits Congress to designate the national coinage, prescribe the weight and fineness, and guarantee its authenticity. Instead of guaranteeing an honest unit of account (an absolute necessity for a healthy economy) Congress, with help from the Federal Reserve, has guaranteed its destruction through official counterfeiting.

George Read, representing Delaware at the Constitutional Convention, wanted the power to "emit bills of credit" to be stricken from the document. He thought the words, if not removed, would be as alarming as "the mark of the beast" in Revelations.

John Langdon of New Hampshire felt equally as strong about the issue, saying he would rather reject the whole plan than retain the power to create paper money.

The strong motivation of the framers of the Constitution, in limiting money to gold and silver coinage, was to restore confidence in American money after the tragic events associated with the continental dollar.

In 1792, the Coinage Act defined the dollar as 371-1/4 grains of fine silver. Mistakenly, the Act also fixed the price of gold to silver at 15-to-1. This concept, called bimetallism, plus fractional reserve banking, played havoc with the monetary system throughout the nineteenth century.

In 1834 the ratio of gold to silver was changed to 16-to-1. But this kind of price-fixing between two commodities cannot work. Depending on the market, either gold or silver will be overvalued and tend to disappear from circulation. And that is exactly what happened periodically.

Today the free market places the ratio much higher. A sound system needs only to define the unit of account in one of the precious metals, preferably gold, and the market can adjust the ratio of one to the other on a daily basis.

Early Challenges to Gold—the Transition

The argument that gold is not practical due to the problems of the nineteenth century is not legitimate. Bimetallism and state and private bank inflation were responsible for the problem. Twice we saw attempts at establishing a central bank, the First and Second Banks of the United States. Thomas Jefferson ended the First Bank of the United States and Andrew Jackson ended the Second, and up until 1913, we did quite well without one.

We must remember it was the government's abuse of the gold standard and bank privilege that gave us our booms and busts on which the anti-gold people of today blame capitalism and gold. Frequently during war, governments abandon the gold standard in order to inflate the currency to pay the bills. This was certainly true during our Civil War, even though the Constitution gives no authority to inflate and strictly prohibits anything but gold and silver from being used as money. This Civil War suspension was the first time since the adoption of the Constitution that our government had tried to make paper legal tender, and it prompted the historic legal tender cases.

Chief Justice Salmon Chase in one of the legal tender cases said:

> Most unquestionably there is no legal tender and there can be no legal tender in this country under the authority of this government of any other but gold and silver, either the coinage of our mints or foreign coins at rates regulated by Congress. This is a constitutional principle perfectly plain and of the very highest importance. The states are prohibited from making anything but gold and silver a tender in payments of debt, and although no such expressed prohibition to Congress, as yet Congress has no power granted to it in this respect but to coin money and regulate the value of foreign coin. Con-

> gress has no power to substitute paper or anything else for a coin as a tender in payment of debts and in discharge of contracts.

Since Congress has no power other than that which is authorized by the Constitution, it's obvious that it has neither power nor authority to make paper legal tender as it has done for the last seventy-five years.

Throughout the nineteenth century, the U.S. maintained a gold standard, although imperfectly. Anytime the system was abused, cooler minds prevailed and we returned to gold. This always involved a cost, and panics and crashes occurred periodically. However, the government followed a hands-off economic policy during the nineteenth century and the corrections were swift.

Even the major changes after the Civil War, with the return to gold convertibility on January 1, 1879, were done smoothly. The philosophy of runaway deficits had not yet been accepted by the people, and the people trusted their elected officials.

Finally, the Panic of 1907 was instrumental in getting the U.S. Congress to pass the Federal Reserve Act of 1913. Instead of the swift correction characteristic of the nineteenth century, the Federal Reserve Act ushered in the age of great depressions, rapid inflation, and massive government interventionism in the marketplace.

After the Wall Street panic of October 1907, there was a cry for reform of the monetary system. The financial manipulators saw their chance to establish a central bank whose control would be "private" and uninhibited by congressional action. The deal was struck that if the central bank accommodated congressional spending, Congress would leave the bank alone in its control of the money. Public pressure prevented total control over money and credit all at once, but the plans were laid for the disintegration of the gold standard which was finalized in August 1971, fifty-eight years after the passage of the Federal Reserve Act.

The Monetary Control Act of 1980 codified the powers that the Fed assumed over the years and filled the vacuum created by gold's dethronement. This law greatly enhanced the powers of the Federal Reserve and made the problems of central banking worse.

It's more than a coincidence that the money supply, as measured by M1 (cash and checking account deposits), has more than tripled since 1971; gold has gone up more than tenfold. And yet the most serious problems inherent in central banking have only begun in the United States.

The Origins of the Fed

The Federal Reserve cartelizes the banking industry, allowing individual banks to inflate together, earning them and the government enormous profits, while making sure that they are never held accountable for their fraudulent practices.

The Federal Reserve cartelizes the banking industry

Here's how we got saddled with this monstrosity: In the early 1900s—during the so-called Progressive Era— the U.S. government began a radical program of intervention into the economy. Pundits hailed this as fostering a new "spirit of cooperation" between business and government. In fact, the new system was a precursor of socialism and fascism.

Government-business cooperation took several forms, all of which conferred special privileges on favored firms, insulating them from the competition of the free market. Individual businesses and whole industries lobbied and bribed government officials for laws that benefited them at the expense of the consumer, and the whole operation was sold to the public as anti-monopoly measures. This illegitimate and unconstitutional process happened time and time again, and government intervention became a permanent part of manufacturing, railroads, agriculture, and many other industries in the U.S.

This was the era when the U.S. free market received a beating and, for lovers of liberty, its effect was much worse than the New Deal's.

In the free market, opportunity is granted to all and privilege to none. Laws affect all equally, businesses seek to meet the needs of the people, and the consumer is king. But in a system of government intervention, industries are no longer accountable to the needs of the people. They receive special privilege and status from the State. They are guaranteed profits, prices, and sales. Liberated from the dictates of the people, businesses are free to indulge themselves in plundering consumers. These were the years of many evils: the income tax, "making the world safe for democracy" through World War I, centralization through direct election of Senators, the imperial Presidency, Prohibition, and the Federal Reserve System.

Academics, as is still the case, provided intellectual cover for these crimes. Thornton Cooke, writing in the pro-big-government *American Economic Review* in 1911, explained why banking needs to be centralized: "American banking has made little use of the principle of cooperation, yet for a generation that principle has been the greatest single factor in American economics." The railroads have their "community of interest arrangements" and manufacturing "has been integrated" so now, he said, it's time to consolidate banking.

But in a system of government intervention, industries are no longer accountable to the needs of the people.

Cooke was arguing for a government-enforced banking cartel, similar to the railroad industry's. The new "collective spirit" of the American economy naturally leads to centralizing money and credit to argue for bank cartelization:

> American banks, however, remain independent, almost isolated units. The effect of isolation has been heightened by the lack of power in any of the 2,300 units to issue a credit note. It is unnecessary to rehearse the arguments showing that our bank note currency is absolutely inelastic...There is not one country bank, however small, that has assurance that any correspondent, however large, is powerful enough to save it if it needs saving in a general panic.

Cooke's arguments were typical, repeated again and again, by promoters of the Fed. They said: the current system was inadequate, it was out-of-step with the times, it caused banker isolation, and most importantly, bankers needed stronger guarantees of monetary inflation when it was needed; i.e. they wanted bailouts and guaranteed profits.

About the then-current National Banking System (NBS), Cooke was lying. In fact a true gold standard monetary system with almost-free banking had not existed since two decades before the Civil War. The NBS actually represented a halfway point between free banking and central banking. And it did have problems, but these existed because of the government.

Chiefly responsible for passing the National Banking Act of 1863 was

Ohio investment banker Jay Cooks, who gained a government-granted monopoly on public debt underwriting. His success in the bond business gained him enormous influence with the Republican Administrations during the Civil War and after, and especially with Salmon Chase, Secretary of the Treasury from Ohio and Senator John Sherman from Ohio. Together they were able to push through Congress and past the public the National Banking Acts, all of which would benefit banking tremendously. Fractional reserve banking was guaranteed by the government at 15 and 25 percent reserves. A 10 percent annual tax on state bank note issues was required, to force state banks into the NBS. Legal tender status was imposed on the National bank notes.

There was plenty of government intervention in the banking system already. The banks were not "isolated" and independent, as the advocates of the Federal Reserve Act suggested.

Because of a general dissatisfaction with the NBS, banking reform movements began to emerge in the 1890s. Most historical accounts tend to concentrate on the political movements for reform, like the pro-inflation free-silver position of Bryanite populism and the arguments for the "correct" gold/silver ratio. The future, though, did not lie with these political movements. The reform to follow was more far-reaching and more fundamental.

Most of these vocal political movements had died out and were rejected by both parties by 1914. From the beginning of the debate, the business and banking community who wanted cartelization opposed the agenda of the political movements without any equivocation. Bankers wanted reform of the banking system, but of their own kind, for their own ends.

Many proposals for monetary reform were presented to Congress after the NBS-generated monetary panic of 1893, all of them designed by elements within the banking community. There was ignorance concerning the complexities of banking from virtually every other sector. Typical was Theodore Roosevelt who, like many politicians, bragged of his ignorance saying: "I do not intend to speak...on the financial question because I am not clear what to say..." Among the first to call for a modern totally centralized bank was Lyman J. Gage, President McKinley's Secretary of the Treasury and former president of the American Bankers Association.

The central banking movement began to grow a year before the Panic of 1907 in New York. Jacob H. Schiff, an investment banker, persuaded the New York Chamber of Commerce to advocate banking reform.

A committee was established, led by the most powerful investment and commercial bankers in New York, which concluded that the solution lay in establishing a central bank "similar to the Bank of Germany." The Chairman of the Board of Chase National Bank (now Chase Manhattan), A. Barton Hepburn, came next with his plan. He did not openly advocate a central bank; he urged creating regional clearing-houses that would issue bond-secured currency in varying amounts. These would be guaranteed by a common fund built up by taxes on the notes.

The Panic of 1907 brought about a sudden loss of confidence in the banking system, and the bankers seized the moment. Not everyone, however, wanted further centralization. *The New York Times,* standing alone, concluded that government intervention in the economy at all levels was responsible for the loss of confidence. Their opposition to a central bank was snuffed out. They were, of course, speaking against the desires of the Establishment of powerful businessmen and bankers.

The *Times* polled Congress and found that they were either thoroughly confused, had a limited understanding over monetary affairs, or that their proposals were too vague to characterize. The *Times* did find, though, there was a consensus that any changes should be in the direction of an "intimate connection between the currency and legitimate trade." They wanted "elasticity," the ability to inflate on demand. Into this vacuum stepped influential bankers.

In 1908 Congress passed a bill similar to Hepburn's plan called the Aldrich-Vreeland Act. (Senator Nelson Aldrich [R-RI] was the son-in-law of John D. Rockefeller.) It was established as a temporary measure to provide liquidity during emergencies. It wasn't used until after the Federal Reserve was established six years later, so the measure was relatively insignificant. But it did contain a clause that would prove to be highly significant. It called for a National Monetary Commission to study the National Banking System and make recommendations for future monetary reform.

The National Monetary Commission (NMC) was comprised of nine senators and nine representatives. Heading up the commission, holding the seat as chairman, was Nelson Aldrich, Rockefeller's "man" in the Senate. As with most congressional commissions, much of the work was done by intellectuals and powerful figures from outside Congress who came in to help with research and writing. Among these were Henry P. Davison, a J.P. Morgan-partner, and George M. Reynolds, president of the American Bankers Association.

Also associated directly or indirectly with the NMC were the most vocal advocates of centralized banking reform: O.M.W. Sprague of Harvard, Edwin W. Kemmerer of Princeton, M.L. Muhleman, James Laurence Laughlin of the University of Chicago, H. Parker Willis of Washington & Lee University, Thornton Cooke, William A. Scott and many others.

The Commission produced a huge pro-central-bank document, assumed to be definitive, though really a boring monetary history under the National Banking System. The document's real function was to serve as the unanswerable critique of the status quo. Today, the Federal Reserve's own *Purposes and Functions of the Federal Reserve System* identifies the Commission's research as the primary historical case for establishing the Federal Reserve.

The Commission was given an unlimited budget and broad investigative power, and they used them in part to travel to Europe to observe their central banking systems. It was during these travels that Senator Aldrich educated himself about the intricacies of central banking and became an open advocate of central banking.

The bankers themselves were not unified on the *precise* nature of the reform they wanted. And by 1909, as an issue, banking reform discussion was limited to a small segment of the banking community. The bankers searched the whole year for a unified plan which they could support, and by the end of that year, they emerged unified. Their communications were generally aired through the *Banking Law Journal.*

Several ingredients tied all reform plans together: central banking, the ability to inflate, and regional banking centers of the type endorsed by the American Banking Association. Also important among the bankers was avoiding the appearance of a banking system controlled by Wall Street. This was a strategic move designed to avoid the strong anti-Wall Street sentiment in America at that time.

During 1910 the issue would have been dormant were it not for the influence of Paul M. Warburg, who played a primary role in establishing the Fed. He emigrated from Germany and became a member of the distinguished banking house of Kuhn, Loeb and Co. Long an advocate of central banking, his behind-the-scenes work propelled the NMC toward the direction of the German banking experience.

Warburg argued, as do current advocates of central banking, that certain sectors of the economy are unnecessarily strained during some seasons but not in others. For example, he argued, certain crops like wheat are harvested seasonally, and merchants and buyers are strained for sufficient cash to purchase what they might need for supplying the commodity during the upcoming months. The farmers then sell the wheat for below-market prices, "dumping" it, which ultimately causes cyclical price fluctuations within the market for crucial commodities. These market fluctuations cause losses in all sectors, producers and sellers, and provide a disincentive to produce.

Inflating the money supply benefits the banker who is in charge of distributing credit

Would an emergency currency help solve the problem? As Warburg says in his 1907 pamphlet "A Plan for a Modified Central Bank," it would not because during a crisis "the run of the depositors would have been carried into the ranks of the note holders, to the disaster of the entire money system. "The answer he says lies in patterning the American banking system after the European model, in which money as credit is centralized and circulating notes are issued against sound commercial paper. These notes would meet the additional demand during seasonal changes, and the amount would naturally contract as the obligations are paid off.

As Warburg explained:

> Most of the paper taken by the American banks still consists of simple promissory notes, which rest only on the credit of the merchant who makes the notes, and which are kept until maturity by the bank or corporation that discounts them. If discounted at all they are generally passed on without endorsement, and the possibility of selling any note depends on the chance of finding another bank which may be willing to give the credit. The consequence is that while in Europe the liquid assets of the banks consist chiefly of bills receivable, long and short, which thus constitute their quickest assets, the American bank capital invested in commercial notes is virtually immobilized.

The proposal was then for a modified central bank, with shares to be owned half by the U.S. government and half by the national banks, and a capital base of $50-100 million ($1 billion in real terms). The bank would be a depository for the Treasury and also be a bank's bank. It would be able to issue notes of legal tender status. These notes would circulate the process of banks' exchanging them for commercial paper endorsed by a member bank—limiting the number that could circulate at any given time. The commercial paper itself could also serve as money, if doubly and triply secured by the endorsement of the bank. It would do so by the individual bank itself issuing a note verifying the holding of such commercial paper. This eventually became the foundation of the Federal Reserve system.

The bankers, by now more properly called Banksters, wanted the ability to inflate together uniformly. Why inflate? In the same way counterfeiting benefits the counterfeiter, so inflating the money supply benefits the banker who is in charge of distributing credit.

Warburg as much as admitted that was their goal:

> We need some centralized power to protect us against others and to protect us from ourselves—some power able to provide for the legitimate needs of the country and able at the same time to apply the brakes when the car is moving too fast.

Under his system, he assures us, banking crises would be minimized, if noticed at all.

> Whatever causes may have precipitated the...crisis [Panic of 1907], it is certain that they never could have brought about the outrageous conditions, which fill us with horror and shame, if we had had a modern bank and currency system.

Further, he argued, America was way behind, and to keep up with "modern" banking methods, the National Banking System put America "at the same point that had been reached by Europe at the time of the Medicis, and by Asia, in all likelihood, at the time of Hammurabi."

Warburg always insisted his plan did not provide for a central bank, but rather a "modified" version. His plan, though, contained the elements considered to be part of centralization: all reserves would be controlled by central authority, enforced through governmental, i.e., coercive, means.

Warburg's brother-in-law became the chief advocate of the plan, Edwin R.A. Seligman of the investment banking family J. & W. Seligman and Company. Seligman was chiefly responsible for assuring the public that Warburg's plan did not involve total bank centralization and that his modified version would not be controlled by Wall Street. (A poll recently showed 59 percent of the bankers wanted a system that appeared to be free from "Wall Street or any monopolistic Interest.")

During the year 1910, the NMC was releasing its proposals for monetary reform. Their plan bore remarkable resemblance to Warburg's. It called for substantial backing of notes with commercial paper rather than public or private bonds, and banks would obtain money through sale or rediscount of "notes and bills of exchange drawn for agricultural, industrial, or commercial purposes, and not including notes or bills issued or drawn for the purpose of carrying stocks, bonds, or other investment purposes."

The new bank, the National Reserve Association, was to issue notes secured by one-half gold, and a technical provision would allow banks to back currency with U.S. Government bonds at par value to the extent of half their value. This little-noticed provision would later become the basis of open market operations in the Federal Reserve System.

The authority over the quality maintenance of notes would rest entirely with the NRA. On the issue of the quantity of notes in circulation, the Commission again adopted the view of Warburg: market demand for money would determine that by member banks' rediscounting their commercial paper with the National Reserve Association and issuing notes on that basis. The paper would mature and the notes expire after demand returned to normal.

The only disagreement that occurred between the conferees at Jeckyll Island was over the issue of partial or total centralization

---

The Commission offered a seventeen-point criticism—with alternatives—of the then-current banking system. They complained, for example, that the current system "has no provision for the concentration of cash reserves of the banks and for their mobilization and use wherever needed in time of trouble." What they tried to make appear as a shortcoming was actually a blessing, as we now know.

Rockefeller and Warburg played a greater role in the drafting of the Commission's actual bill than providing passive intellectual influence. Just before the release of NMC's final legislative recommendations, someone associated with Aldrich (no one knows who) proposed getting all leading big bankers and advocates of banking reform together for a secret meeting and drafting a bill. The super-secret meeting was to be held at the Jeckyll Island Club in Georgia. The press reported only that they were going there for a duck-hunting expedition. The members all assumed names and traveled on a private railroad.

During that week at the luxury resort, the bill that the Commission would release (what would later become the Federal Reserve Act) was drafted. Among the shady participants at the important Jeckyll Island meeting were:

Senator Nelson W. Aldrich (Rockefeller in-law)
Henry P. Davison (Morgan partner)
Paul M. Warburg (Kuhn Loeb & Co.)
Frank A. Vanderlip (VP of Rockefeller's National City Bank)
Charles D. Norton (president of Morgan's First National Bank of New York)
A. Piat Andrew (Harvard economist, assistant to Aldrich on the National Monetary Commission, and banking expert)

The result of this meeting was the Commission's bill, the Aldrich Plan, the basis of the Federal Reserve Act. The only disagreement that occurred between the conferees at Jeckyll Island was over the issue of partial or total centralization. All wanted total centralization, but some were more politically astute than others and knew that Congress would never approve of a totally banker-controlled central bank.

Senator Aldrich, who strangely did not understand why centralization could not be presented outright, was overridden by the more politically astute Warburg, who endorsed the Morawetz version of regional banking centers under the cover of decentralization. The board of directors in the original Aldrich plan was to be chosen solely by bankers, but that was later changed in the spirit of decentralization to make half of them appointed by the President of the United States.

The bill was delayed for one year and finally presented before the Congress in January 1912 so that support for the bill could be consolidated. This was done by means of a conference in Atlantic City during February 1911 where 22 top bankers met to discuss the Aldrich Plan. It was warmly endorsed with the resolution written by Paul Warburg. As Gabriel Kolko says: "Indeed, the plan was endorsed at the outset. The real purpose of the conference was to discuss winning the banking community over to government control directed the bankers for their own ends."

There was still the stigma of the bill's being the product of Wall Street, Rockefeller interests, and Senator Aldrich. To solve the problem, Warburg and other New York bankers created the National Citizens' League for the Promotion of a Sound Banking System. This would be a "grassroots" lobbying group headed up by economist J. Laurence Laughlin of the University of Chicago. Its purpose was "to carry on an active campaign for monetary reform on the general principles of the Aldrich Plan without endorsing every detail. "This, of course, wasn't a "grassroots" movement. It was a get-rich-quick scheme promoted by the top-brass bankers in the country.

For the first time, during the year 1911, academic, economic, and banking journals were, for the first time, overflowing with praise for the Aldrich Plan. In June, William Scott of the University of Wisconsin wrote that the Aldrich Plan would solve the "most fundamental defects in our currency system, namely: its lack of elasticity; the uneconomical use of banking reserves, their connection with the stock market, and their control by Wall Street." The Plan would "...greatly increase the efficiency of our banking reserves" and would eliminate the "evil effects of our present independent Treasury system."

According to Scott:

> Persons who suspect that any measure proposed by Senator Aldrich must necessarily be designed to play into the hands of 'the interests' will look for a joker in his plan. They will have considerable difficulty, however, in finding it.

Further:

> Wall Street could control the new institution only by absolutely controlling a majority of the banks that will purchase stock in the new institution, and even then its control would be tempered by the influence of the Federal Government...which will be great.

So the plan should be adopted because it would "complete and perfect our present national banking system...." It is, therefore, clear that the articles contained all the information thought most important by the League, Rockefeller, and Warburg.

Strange, isn't it, that an academic journal wouldn't concentrate primarily on debating the economic virtues and vices of the Fed, but would concentrate on selling it to the public?

In the same issue, Harvard economist O.M.W. Sprague, closely aligned with the Commission, called the Plan an "equitable means of banking reform" that reflects "the skillful handiwork of its experienced author." Every specific objection or fear which has been expressed...has been successfully met." The rest of the article was spent arguing for the placement of some regional banks in the West to insure that Wall Street would not control the new institution, once again reflecting what Warburg and Aldrich saw as the main obstacle to bank cartelization: the public's fear of Wall Street.

Thorton Cooke's echo argued for the plan in the same manner. He had glowing praise for the plan and assured the reader that "Wall Street cannot 'make money' out of the activities of the Association." The bank will only "furnish sufficient reserve of credit for ordinary seasonal needs," just as Warburg argued.

In May of that year, the American Bankers Association approved the Aldrich Plan and endorsed a broader number of notes eligible for rediscounting.

Only later in the year did a split occur within the ranks. The split was not over the goals of cartelizing the banking industry, of course, but again over political tactics of doing so. President of the Citizen's League J. Laurence Laughlin was a political realist and knew that Aldrich's name had to be removed from the bill. H. Parker Willis, his good friend and close aide, had warned him about this earlier and now Laughlin was convinced. Even Warburg later separated himself in public from the name Aldrich but, of course, this had no bearing on the facts.

The Aldrich plan was presented to Congress in January of 1912, but with Aldrich about to retire and the Democrats about to win a victory later in the year, the bill never came to a vote; and banking reform was a dead issue for awhile.

The Citizens League continued, though, to function as a powerful and large-scale propagandist for banking reform, issuing pamphlets and brochures all over the country, especially in the South and West, educating people on the evils of the National Banking System and the benefits of centralized banking reform and a conglomerate banking cartel.

The League's periodical "banking reform" was made into a book with 23 chapters dealing with all aspects of banking reform, but 11 were written by H. Parker Willis, a student of Laughlin's, who received $1,000 (over $9,100 in real terms). Willis had taught at Washington and Lee University, and two of his ex-students recommended Parker to their father to be his administrative assistant. Their father was Carter Glass of Virginia, ranking member of the House Committee on Banking and Currency. Willis accepted. Glass needed an assistant for two reasons: first he had no technical knowledge of the banking business, and secondly, he was given responsibility of considering monetary reform and working against the efforts of Arsene P. Pujo to assign the problem of banking reform to the Pujo Subcommittee who was soon to hold hearings on the "Money Trust."

In June of 1912, Willis drew up a bill for Glass and reported to Laughlin in a letter: "After a good deal of talk with Mr. Glass, I drew up a bill along the lines of which you and I spoke, and turned it into him." The Pujo committee swung into high gear with its investigation into alleged abuse of power emanating from Wall Street. The result, though inconclusive, was to stir the public into a frenzy over Wall Street.

Through some remarkable "spin control," the new Glass legislation (the Fed bill) was promoted as an anti-Wall Street bill, building on a foundation established earlier with the Aldrich Bill. The Pujo Committee never won the legislative control from the Glass Committee, which still left Glass (i.e., Willis, Laughlin, and ultimately Warburg) in charge of the bill.

A final bill setting up the Federal Reserve was passed in December 1913 by a large majority in the House (the Aldrich Plan and the Glass bill were virtually identical). As Kolko says:

The entire banking reform movement, at all crucial stages, was centralized in the hands of a few men who for years were linked, ideologically and personally, with one another...the major function, inspiration, and direction of the measure was to serve the banking community in general, and large bankers specifically.

Who authored the bill? No one knows. The controversy sprang up immediately but was never resolved.

H. Parker Willis later denounced the institution of the Federal Reserve and its inflationary policies and became extremely critical just prior to the great depression. Laughlin also attacked the Fed during his later years, although like Willis, not to the extent of repudiating his own role in its establishment.

There is one reason why we have a Federal Reserve System today, and it has nothing to do with what the Fed's publications say. The Federal Reserve exists to give a special privilege to the banking industry. And they have profited greatly from it. But at what expense? The banksters have deluded the value of the 1914 dollar to about eight cents. And its value is still shrinking.

As the Federal Reserve expands the money supply, it reduces the value of all existing dollars. The process happens, though, unevenly because not all prices rise at the same time. The first party to get the new money can spend it at its old purchasing power. Only after filtering through the economy does the money bid up prices for goods.

The Federal Reserve exists to give a special privilege to the banking industry

---

But who gets the new money first? Who experiences the boon from the credit injection? The bankers and Insiders, of course.
They wouldn't have it any other way.

As Ludwig von Mises has shown, the Federal Reserve is responsible for the business cycle as we know it today. With credit injections, the Fed lowers interest rates causing businessmen to invest in new capital equipment. They produce goods that consumers can't afford, and they eventually find that their plans don't pan out. This process spreads throughout the entire economy and creates ever-growing waves of booms and busts. A gold standard economy wouldn't have such a problem.

There is no economic, constitutional, or moral justification for giving special privilege to big bankers over the rest of business or industry. They should be subject to competition in the free market, and the legal constraints against fraud, like everyone else.

The Nature of Money

According to Ludwig von Mises:

> The gold standard makes the determination of money's purchasing power independent of the changing ambitions and doctrines of political parties and pressure groups. This is not a defect of the gold standard, it is its main excellence...What governments call international monetary cooperation is concerted action for the sake of credit expansion.

The most important role money plays is that of a medium of exchange. It also serves as a measurement and storage of value. Money, according to Mises, must originate in the market as a useful commodity in order to function properly.

The most acceptable liquid commodity always becomes money. The particular commodity has varied from culture to culture, but gold has been overwhelmingly chosen as the favorite with silver a close second. Even today in an age of official gold hatred, we find gold is held in huge amounts by the central banks of the world as well as the International Monetary Fund.

Whenever I proposed the public sale of the treasury gold or the return of the IMF gold to the United States, the paper-money advocates correctly retorted that they could not give up the gold because it was the government's only asset.

Politicians may warp a monetary system to their liking but they cannot repeal economic laws that determine the nature of money. Truth about money cannot be changed by legislative shenanigans. Distortion and corruption through monopoly control can benefit the few at the expense of many for long periods of time, but eventually the irrefutable laws of nature will win. In the process of monetary debasement and the subsequent resurgence of commodity money, tragically, a great price must be paid by many innocent people. If we fail to recognize the serious importance of money, the reforms needed will be delayed and the suffering prolonged. However, an opportunity is presenting itself since the system no longer can endure, and the necessity of monetary reform is upon us.

Commodity money is precisely defined and has real value. This makes economic calculation and modern commerce possible. When money is depreciated and its value deliberately destroyed by increasing its supply, we have inflation, and prices go up. This creates conditions which are not as bad as if we had no money at all, but much worse than if we had a commodity money. Continued inflation will eventually reach a stage, if policies are not changed, where the dollar will not function and we will be forced back to bartering regardless of our desires. Then the conditions will become worse.

Money, when its value varies dramatically due to government manipulation of its supply, fails in its key role as a medium of exchange and as the common denominator in economic calculations. The more severe the inflation, the greater the difficulty encountered.

Man's ingenuity is remarkable for adjusting to the changing value of money in the short run. In the long run it gets more difficult. If inflation is getting out of control and the monetary managers refuse, as they usually do, to stop the inflation, politicians inevitably resort to wage and price controls, the worst thing they can do. The conditions that result from controls are similar to those existing as if we had no money at all. Bartering then will be resorted to and black markets will arise, since money's function of serving as the medium of exchange has been removed.

The nature of money must be understood. Just as the press cannot operate without freedom of speech, the economy cannot operate without a sound monetary system.

Even though today's price inflation is still considered moderate, more and more citizens are resorting to bartering services and goods domestically and internationally. Our tax code and IRS harassment encourages this activity, but the difficulty in calculating business transactions with an unstable money and an international-floating-exchange rate accelerates this trend.

Money must be part of a whole concept of freedom and consistent with it; it cannot be separate. When prevailing political and economic attitudes promote deficit financing on a grand scale, along with government economic planning, sound honest money is impossible.

Sound money is characteristic of a free society and a market economy. Under a dictatorship and socialism, government force backed by a gun can pretend to dictate production, regulate distribution, set prices, and force its citizens to use anything it wants--even pieces of paper for money.

When a society accepts irredeemable fiat money, one can be sure the fundamentals of freedom itself are being threatened, and it's only a matter of time before an abusive dictatorship emerges that controls all aspects of our lives if the concept of fiat money is not rejected.

Under the chaotic conditions that result from inflation of the money supply, government force substitutes for the practical and peaceful method of setting prices in distributing goods. All decisions become political, not economic, and reason and justice are both rejected.

Ludwig Von Mises was the first to show that socialism cannot achieve the very complex calculation required to establish a market price. Free choice in the market is the only way economic calculation can come about. The market is remarkable and can overcome great obstacles placed in its way by government manipulation of the money supply, but it cannot do this indefinitely.

F. A. Hayek, another great Austrian economist and student of Mises, was asked if he thought the United States would experience runaway inflation as seen in Europe in the past:

> Oh, I believe I can assure you that you'll never get hyperinflation in the sense in which the Germans experienced it. You'll probably get something much worse. You see, an open inflation in which prices are allowed to adjust themselves to an increase in the quantity of money, is a very great nuisance and very disturbing. But so long as the market is allowed to determine prices, the economy can still function.
>
> There is something much worse than an open inflation and I'm afraid that's what you're headed for, a continued increase in the quantity of money with government prohibitions against price rises—"repressed inflation" as I like to call it. This is a situation in which the process of monetary expansion continues, but government clamps down on one price after another, believing that it can disguise inflation by not allowing prices to rise.
>
> Hitler followed this practice throughout his regime. Despite the colossal monetary expansion, prices remain constant because people were shot if they raised prices. As a result the whole self-ordering system of the market was suspended. Instead of having to pay higher prices, people had to submit to a rationing system. It meant not getting things at all rather than having to pay higher prices for them. You are probably marching into such a system of wage and price controls, where prices and wages cease to be appropriate guides for economic activity; where scarcities no longer manifest themselves in high prices but in nonavailability of what you want. It will be rationing by ration tickets instead of cash in your pockets.

We already see this happening in the United States with the distribution of government-paid hospital care.

Even though the market adjusts to government increases in the money supply, it cannot do so indefinitely, nor can it do so fairly. Although current market mechanics permit the economy to function, avoiding complete economic collapse, these adjustments cannot prevent distortion and unfair transfer of wealth that continually gnaws away at the social fabric. With a sound currency and market economy, everyone who is honestly seeking a living benefits and only those looking for a shortcut to riches suffer.

If tampering with the money supply affected everyone equally—as was supposed before Mises demonstrated differently—and if price controls were never imposed, the detrimental effects would be limited indeed. However, this is not the case, for one group always benefits at the expense of another under the condition of inflation. It never serves the general welfare to inflate a currency, but it does benefit power. Even though this is the case, exact predictions as to who and to what degree each group will benefit or suffer are not possible.

Money had always been thought to be "neutral" and the price of a product depended only on the supply and the demand of the goods sold. The supply of money was not thought to be critical in determining the specific price. This was even tacitly accepted by the early Austrian economists, but it took Mises to prove the non-neutrality of money. It was thought that if money were neutral and the money supply changed, all prices changed simultaneously. This is the current monetarist view.

This very important fact is critical because it explains why inflation becomes a tool of the special interest and is so unfair. It also tells why it is so destructive and yet so persistent. Mises explains:

> A change in purchasing power of money causes prices of different commodities and services to change neither simultaneously nor evenly, in that it is incorrect to maintain the changes in the quantity of money brings about simultaneous and proportional changes in the level of prices.

Expanding on this in his great book *Human Action*, Mises says:

> As money can never be neutral and stable in purchasing power, a government's plan concerning the determination of the quantity can never be impartial and fair to all members of society. Whatever a government does in the pursuit of aims to influence the height of purchasing power depends necessarily upon the ruler's personal value judgments. It always furthers the interest of some groups of peoples at the expense of other groups. It never serves what is called the common wheel or the public welfare.

When money is manipulated at will by the politicians, it always leads to chaos, unemployment, and political upheaval. For this reason it is imperative that we identify a money that cannot be abused, that prohibits inflation, and allows responsible working citizens to prosper, not the deceitful.

Dr. Murray Rothbard says that one of the world's most important lessons to learn is the simple fact that, "Money is a commodity," and this commodity is unique in that it is demanded mainly as a "medium of exchange."

Either the money managers in Washington today have never learned this basic fact or they think they can defy the economic imperative that says we must have a commodity for money or face inflationary chaos.

It is generally said that money must also measure and store value; yet these are simple functions supporting the one essential function of money—acting as a medium of exchange. Prices are expressed in money and not measured by it. Money's essential attribute is that it facilitates trade by acting as a medium of exchange, and if it is an honest money, it will convey trust and confidence and allow price adjustments of various goods and services in relationship to each other to occur smoothly, efficiently, and fairly.

With sound money, the unit of account is stable and precisely defined; the goal is not to seek rigid prices. Ironically, all monetary managers seek stable prices with their policies and they give us instability, where sound money ignores the goal of stable prices and yet it gives us great stability with growth.

The main purpose of money is not to measure and store value, but to act as a medium of exchange. When fiat money circulates, as it does today, gold helps individuals to survive by storing value. However, if an honest currency circulated, there would be no need for gold to be hoarded. It would be more advantageous to invest this capital than to hide it.

To tamper with a nation's money is to tamper with every economic aspect of every citizen's life: how one gets paid, how much one saves, and what one pays in nominal terms for every purchase made. The business cycle is now understood, thanks to the work of the Austrian economists, to be due solely to the manipulation of the supply of money and credit by the central bank. Therefore, the availability of jobs, the rate of unemployment, the standard of living, are all a reflection in large part of the monetary policy a nation pursues.

Since inflation—the deliberate depreciation of the money—causes serious international trade problems, and protectionism is characteristic of an age of inflation, it can be said that sound money goes a long way toward preventing international conflicts.

Inflation and nationalism have not yet gotten so serious as to provoke hostilities as occurred in the 1930s, but inflation is a common tool for the financing, in a deceitful way, of unpopular wars. War, when just and in the national interest, and supported by the people, will be paid for through legitimate borrowing from the people or through taxation, not through inflation. With sound money, it would be impossible to fight undeclared, unpopular wars such as Vietnam.

In all free societies, or relatively free societies, when the people are permitted a choice, they always choose commodity money over paper.

The question that must be answered in attempting to secure a sound monetary system for a nation: Is it essential that commodity money be used and fiat money be rejected? The overwhelming historic evidence says that the answer to this question is Yes.

In dictatorships, where there is no personal liberty, fiat money can be used. But under totalitarianism sound money serves no economic benefit because in non-market economies, economic calculations are impossible anyway. For this reason there is no practical reason for dictators to have a tool such as sound money for measuring economic value and acting as a medium of exchange. Yet, even under the most oppressive dictatorships, market prices can be found in the black market.

In all free societies, or relatively free societies, when the people are permitted a choice, they always choose commodity money over paper. The two, sound money and a free society, go together. Without the one you cannot have the other.

If a market economy tries to operate with an inflating fiat currency, productivity and capital investment become very difficult, if not impossible. As the money is destroyed, government power and interference in the market increase in an attempt to maintain order. Government officials refuse to admit that economic planning does not work until it's too late. And then it becomes obvious that the government's attempt to compensate for "printing too much money" only makes things worse.

Credit allocations, indirect or direct, never achieve that which is intended. For instance, if credit is created to build houses for the poor, the number of poor without houses increases while the shrewd businessman gets wealthier in the process.

The bureaucrats certainly will thrive under these conditions. Deficits, run up for so-called humanitarian purposes, will be monetized with more printing-press money; the hungry will get hungrier, the poor, poorer. The subsequent unemployment and the high prices brought on by these unwise government actions will provoke many to demand more inflation, not realizing inflation was the cause of the problem in the first place.

The worst thing a government can impose on the economy after the politicians become concerned about the mess they have created, is wage and price controls. Controls eliminate the most important role the market plays—economic calculation in the voluntary setting of prices. Controls cannot substitute for the lack of trust in the money.

Money, Liberty, Morality

Sound money is closely related to liberty and morality. Sound money, it might be said, is only possible with liberty, and liberty is, only possible with a high regard for morality.

S. Herbert Frankel, in his excellent essay, "Money and Liberty," credits John Locke as being, "the first to set out the basic moral issues raised by money," by showing that money helps to transfer subsistence economics, and in the process releases man from a narrow dependence on nature. Locke does not separate his views on money from his great interest in personal liberty. Frankel explains this clearly and places proper emphasis on the relationship:

> A second strand in Locke's thought which has unfortunately been largely neglected, is his treatment of money as an essential element in the protection of the free personality of the individual. For Locke, the right to possess, use, and to store up money is fundamental. Like the ownership of property, it is not conferred on the individual by society, but rather civil society has been established to protect this right.

This view is important for a proper understanding of our present monetary difficulties.

Defending individual liberty and money together was essential for Locke, for the two cannot be treated separately. A free society that cannot maintain a sound currency cannot achieve economic growth. Making and keeping contracts requires money of real value, money that can be trusted at home and abroad.

Frankel adds: "For Locke, the right to possess and use money is man's natural right just as it is his natural right to preserve his property, that is, his life, liberty and estate."

Trust, or lack of it, in the money throughout the ages has been a reflection of the government's attitude toward liberty in general and money in particular. When government compels its citizens through legal-tender laws to use a depreciated currency in spite of the continuing erosion of its value, the people eventually catch on and lose trust in the money. When this trust is totally destroyed, economic and political chaos result.

For orderly trade to occur, the monetary unit must have a precise definition in order to prevent wild fluctuations in prices and interest rates. Clearly, the change that the U.S. dollar has gone through in the last two decades certainly cannot be an example of stable money.

From an historical viewpoint, whenever the people had something to say about it, they demanded commodity money.

Trust in money cannot be achieved by hollow government promises to print less money, tax less, spend less, or fix exchange rates. It will require a money that the people control, not the government or the bankers. History proves that governments rarely fulfill their responsibility in maintaining the value of money, whether they gain this power legally or surreptitiously.

Even when gold was used, governments changed the rules and were not always disciplined by it. Even though the nineteenth century was our best example of a time when the world accepted the notion of real money, and governments followed the rules relatively well, our leaders violated this trust and tampered significantly with the money during the Civil War.

From an historical viewpoint, whenever the people had something to say about it, they demanded commodity money. If a government abuses a gold standard, the people react by taking possession of the gold itself, which places restraints on the monetary authorities and calls a halt to the fraud. However, governments knowing this, usually attack personal liberties (as they did in the United States in the 1930s) by prohibiting the private ownership of gold and reneging on its bad gold-clause promises—thus removing the real protection of a gold standard.

The most important characteristic of sound money is the trust associated with it. Even paper money works when the people unknowingly trust it. Lack of trust in the money is translated into what is called "inflationary expectations." This term directs one's thinking to the impending price hikes bound to come in the near and distant future. "Inflationary expectations" would be better called the anticipation that the money will be further destroyed by the arbitrary increase in its quantity by the government. As inflation worsens, more and more people become aware that irresponsible government spending and deficits are the reasons behind the increase in the money supply. Until the people understand and believe that government will mend its ways and live within its means, they will continue to "anticipate that the money will be further destroyed."

When everyone loses trust in the money, the whole system breaks down and currency reform becomes necessary. There is a significant chance that this will happen by the 1990s.

Inflation and the Poor

Henry Hazlitt in *Economics In One Lesson* points out how unfair inflation is to the poor:

> The poor are usually more heavily taxed in percentage terms than the rich, for they do not have the same means for protecting themselves by speculative purchases of real equities... The rate of the tax imposed by inflation is not a fixed one: it cannot be determined in advance...
>
> Like every other tax, inflation acts to determine the individual and business policies we are forced to follow. It discourages all prudent thrift. It encourages squandering, gambling, and reckless waste of all kinds. It often makes it more profitable to speculate than to produce. It tears apart the whole fabric of stable economic relationships. Its inexcusable injustices drive men toward desperate remedies. It

> plants the seeds of fascism and communism. It leads men to demand totalitarian control. It ends invariably in bitter disillusion and collapse.

Even if by some quirk paper money provided a net benefit to the economy, it would still have to be rejected for moral reasons. The power to create credit out of thin air is the moral equivalent to counterfeiting. Applying the Robin Hood ethic, robbing the rich to help the poor, cannot justify the process. Money creation dilutes the value of money already earned. It is a deceitful tax, unseen by all but a few and is equivalent to a farmer diluting his milk supply with water. Counterfeiting is a criminal offense when a private citizen attempts it, and the same rules of conduct should be applied to government or Federal Reserve officials. Inflation never helps the poor as is intended and enriches a special class until the collapse.

There are no-long term benefits to inflation so utilitarians should never be tempted to endorse the system. But since there are short-term benefits to inflation to some special interest groups, this makes the temptation irresistible for the politicians. The pain and suffering that comes from inflation are delayed and scattered, and the victims are rarely aware of what's happening to them—a policy to which politicians easily adapt.

Trust

Maintaining trust in the money is a must, and this can only be done when we have a government that is trustworthy and a money controlled, not by the politicians, but by the people. Trust in money usually lasts longer than one would predict. For instance, today the money has no guaranteed value, yet it functions rather well as money due to the residual trust placed in it. This trust exists out of ignorance, as well as out of false hopes that the government will eventually do something about the problem.

Claims are made that the productive capacity of the nation backs the dollar, but this is nothing more than wishful thinking. If prices soar, there is no way that the currency one holds can be redeemed in something of value. Even though there now is more trust placed in the money than it deserves, at some point, when the people panic, more confusion and chaos will result than would be expected. Prices then can rise even faster than the rate the government is increasing the money supply. In the end the trust in the money is of the utmost importance in determining whether or not the money will function in a useful manner.

Of all symbols that are associated with government, money is one of the most important. Once total loss of this trust occurs, it is followed by economic upheaval and radical social change. Frankel addressed the potential danger:

> For money symbolizes the very matrix of society—the trust or mistrust by which the personal and political interrelations of its members stand or fall. Once trust in money has been lost through whatever circumstances, the freedom of the men and women in society will be correspondingly diminished or ultimately destroyed.

The stakes are high—not only because the economic benefits we all receive are threatened by not having a sound currency with which to trade—but because of the close association between honest money and freedom. Our liberty can be lost as well.

The magnificent feature of a true gold standard is that the government can always be held in check if the people begin to mistrust the government.

In periods of significant inflation, the people are not only disturbed by the untrustworthiness of the system, they become angry at certain groups that benefit or appear to benefit from inflation. The unfairness of inflation's transfer of wealth from one group to another becomes more evident as the inflationary process worsens. The magnificent feature of a true gold standard is that the government can always be held in check if the people begin to mistrust the government.

John Maynard Keynes maintained that the average person should not be allowed to hold gold coins, for this locks up wealth and represents waste. He either never understood the benefits of the gold standard, or he believed power over the economy ought to be placed in the hands of bankers and government officials. Governments have a poor record in limiting the supply of money and are forever yielding to the temptation of financing debt by expanding the money supply. Keynes placed his trust in government rather than in the people and the free-market choice for gold.

Need for Leadership

Another outstanding student of Mises, Hans Sennholz, in his book *The Age of Inflation,* states there are "few tasks, if any...more important to the champion of freedom than the creation of a sound monetary system." There should be no doubt whatsoever of the need and urgency for establishing a sound monetary system in the United States and every other country claiming to be free.

Jacques Rueff, in a 1971 *Barron's* interview, agrees with Sennholz and warns that chances of success are limited even if a political leader is available to us: "If political circumstances prevent him (the leader) from emerging, man's destruction is as inevitable as that of a man falling from the roof of a skyscraper."

Leadership is critical and great changes in history have come about as a result of efforts made by certain individuals. Yet political circumstances and general understanding by the people cannot be ignored.

Today we have an unanswered question of whether or not the welfare ethic and interventionism that promote the inflation system (that so many have grown to love) will preclude making the necessary, and sometimes unpopular, decisions required to preserve freedom and establish sound money.

Motivation

A major reform of our monetary system must come. In order to plan for that reform, we must not only understand the nature of money, but we must understand the motivations of those who promote paper money and inflation.

There are four major reasons why governments and politicians reject gold's discipline and promote paper money:

1. The twentieth century economists have taught three generations of Americans that gold is a relic of the past and fiat money is modern and workable.
2. A gold standard limits government deficit financing and both liberals and conservatives, although for different reasons, need a central bank

to monetize debt.

3. The knowledgeable elite who are in charge of the affairs of state use control of the money to control the wealth of the nation.
4. Ignorance of what money is and how the Federal Reserve operates prompts many citizens and members of Congress to avoid getting involved in the issue.

Economic Reasons

Government intervention in the economy has been an accepted policy throughout most of the twentieth century. The degree of this acceptance was greatly increased during the Great Depression of the 1930s. For fifty years now, essentially all economists teaching at our major universities justified economic intervention, credit creation, and deficit financing. The result is what we have today: a Congress filled with members who know little else, staffers who spout their professor's cliches, and a press that regurgitates the same nonsense.

Interventionism clearly teaches that government programs are necessary to maintain full employment and prosperity. Although the people choose security over self-reliance, the evidence is clear that not only do government programs fail but they are the major source of our problems.

The liberal Keynesians have grabbed the moral high ground, and anyone concerned about his fellow man is made to feel guilty if government intervention is not wholeheartedly endorsed. Sincere, dedicated professors, members of Congress, staffers, and media people promote the nonsense with the best of intentions, believing that economic conditions can be improved through government spending and planning. Very few remember that the fifth plank of the *Communist Manifesto* advocates the monopoly control of money and credit with a powerful central bank.

Keynesian economic beliefs about money are based on the assumption that inflation of the money supply stimulates the economy and true economic growth results.

Even the conservative supply-siders promote similar foolishness, rationalizing in their own mind that balanced budgets are an old-fashioned concept, claiming inflation is not related to the Federal Reserve's monetary policy. Paper money managers are arrogant enough to believe that they can adjust interest rates and control supply and demand to such a degree that a healthy prosperous economy will result. Many who spout this fallacious economic theory sincerely believe it's the best policy to follow for the greatest prosperity and do not do so for personal gain. Regardless of the motivation, however, if the theory is wrong, suffering results nonetheless.

Monetization of Debt

With an honest gold standard, politicians cannot create credit out of thin air to pay for deficit financing. This procedure—when the Federal Reserve accommodates the politicians' spendthrift ways by buying the treasury bills or bonds with credit created out of thin air—is called monetization of debt. History shows that any time this tool is available to politicians, they always abuse it by creating excessive amounts of debt and credit.

The supply-siders, led by Congressman Jack Kemp, are shrewd enough to know that the gold standard is a good political issue. However they are not anxious to use the gold standard in the way it was intended: to control spending, deficits, and credit creation along with the size of government. Supply-siders do not advocate elimination of the Federal Reserve nor its power to monetize debt. Deficits are not a concern of the supply-siders. A supply-side gold standard is correctly called a pseudo or fraudulent gold standard.

This distinction is of utmost importance, because when the time comes that monetary reform is seriously considered, it's crucial that the advocates of the fake gold standard are not in control of the reform.

Deficit financing is the friend of the politician. It permits political promises that assure constituent satisfaction and re-election for the representative. Championing every cause regardless of cost makes it easy for the incumbent to be re-elected. A recent survey of Texas members of Congress, including two Senators, asked them to evaluate their previous year's performance. Both conservative and liberal members bragged either of securing government jobs for the district or influencing policy enough to send more federal funds to their district.

Deficits under a gold standard would have to be paid for directly through borrowing or taxation, causing a more immediate burden on the economy, and would obviously be less popular. Monetizing the debt delays the ill effects of the expanded credit; the victims are not easily identified. The process is popular with both the politicians and their constituents who desire these expensive programs.

Conservatives and liberals both endorse the process of debt monetization, even though they do not agree on particular programs. The coalition of the two, however, guarantees that the Fed's power and its willingness to manage the government deficits will not be challenged by those now representing us in Washington.

For public consumption though, Paul Volcker as chairman of the Fed, routinely chastised the Congress for running huge deficits. Members of Congress never hesitate to do a little Fed-bashing by blaming the central bank for high interest rates, inflation, and recessions.

The truth is that they need each other. The Fed's continued existence and independence depends upon tacit congressional approval, and Congress needs the Fed to monetize the huge deficits.

Conservatives, especially the supply-side hawkish conservatives, need the Fed to finance, indirectly through credit expansion, the military-industrial complex, foreign aid to supposedly loyal allies, international bankers, privileged corporations, expenditures for the infrastructure—dams, highways, ports, bridges etc..

Liberal programs are different, but nonetheless just as expensive. Their programs include: welfare spending, international assistance to left-wing dictators, social programs, federal subsidies to education, and many of the programs conservatives support as well.

The benefits to the politicians of the Federal Reserve's willingness to monetize debt makes it irresistible for them to use it. The fact that it serves both conservatives and liberals means that neither group will ever challenge the system on philosophic principle. It also means that the price we must eventually pay for our extravagance will be delayed.

For this reason we can expect the debt and credit bubble to expand until it bursts sometime in the near future. Understanding the political forces supporting such a system and understanding the economic consequences of such foolishness is crucial to our survival.

Power and Economic Control

The third major reason we have a powerful central bank that maintains monopoly control over credit is that those in charge of policy are granted overwhelming political and economic power. The individuals who, behind the scenes, pull the monetary strings are very much aware of the power they have.

Some have said that the Chairman of the Fed is the second most powerful man in the world, the President being the most powerful. A strong case can be made for the Chairman of the Fed's being more powerful than even the President. The dollar is the reserve currency of the world, and the Chairman has more to say about the dollar than the President. Economic and political events can be endlessly manipulated by U.S. monetary policy. Since our policy is in the hands of dedicated internationalists and the dollar is the international unit of account, world events are totally dependent upon the dollar's value and interest rates.

Third-world debt, foreign aid programs, the IMF, the World Bank, and international trade are all closely related to Federal Reserve policy. Continued monetary inflation to keep the debt system afloat is the essential element of today's policy. Propping up illiquid debtors domestically and internationally by inflation is clearly a process penalizing the innocent middle-class Americans who are being victimized by the process.

Economic law will not permit endless inflation of the money supply without a subsequent increase in prices.

Since nothing in life is ever free, someone has to pay. In this case the middle class suffers through job losses and a lowered standard of living. Both the political and economic elite benefit by accumulation of more power and wealth. The inflationary process allows some to benefit at the expense of others. Since transferring wealth through inflation is more difficult to understand than a direct tax, it continues for long periods of time before it's rejected by the people (who must find new leadership to redirect events.)

Economic benefits accrue to those knowledgeable about Federal Reserve policy. Paul Volcker once admitted to me (to my surprise) before a banking committee hearing, that leaks did indeed occur regarding secret monetary policy. We also clearly know that appointments to the Fed require approval from the international bankers led by David Rockefeller. The key positions are always held by establishment-appointed bankers: the Federal Reserve chairmanship is the presidency of the New York Fed. The president of the New York Fed is always on the Federal Open Market Committee, while other regional presidents rotate their positions on the committee. Frequently, this position is a steppingstone to the chairmanship of the Fed.

Monetary policy can be instrumental in presidential campaigns. The strength of the economy and the level of interest rates can make or break a President seeking reelection. There is clear evidence that monetary policy is frequently manipulated for presidential elections.

Since every transaction is measured in terms of the monetary unit, the power to artificially alter the unit's value literally allows the monetary authorities to control the economy. A free market is very sensitive to freely fluctuating prices and interest rates. The Fed, on an hourly basis, manipulates rates and yet follows an announced policy of stable prices. Of course their goals and their achievements are not always the same, but their efforts play havoc with those honestly trying to make a living without any benefit of inside information.

As powerful as the Fed is, the markets eventually win out. Economic law will not permit endless inflation of the money supply without a subsequent increase in prices. Since gold is the ultimate money of the people, currency depreciation always leads to higher nominal prices for gold and the other precious metals.

The breakdown of international trade eventually comes when enough people discover that the monetary policy is a charade and a fraud. A contest between market forces and government forces then erupts. The name of the game for the monetary authorities is maintaining power over the economy and political events. When paper is rejected by the market, governments inevitably retaliate by enforcing rules regarding currencies, flow of capital, financial privacy, and freedom to travel.

The conflict is already visible and we can expect it to get much worse (including a new paper currency) before it's all over.

The monetary crisis will end when one side is victorious. If paper wins, an authoritarian government will be required. If gold wins, a free society will prevail.

Ignorance and Innocence

Groups that support the Fed for economic reasons are related to those who support the Fed out of ignorance or complacency. Most members of Congress that I know do not have a real understanding of how the process of debt monetization and credit expansion work. The majority of the members do not support the Fed because of strongly held economic beliefs and they don't receive any direct economic or political benefits from it. But neither are they inclined to delve into the complex issue of the Federal Reserve system. Subtly, they probably don't want to know, because the system seems to work and a vague understanding of the Fed still permits demagogic criticism of its policy if that is politically advantageous.

The so-called benefits of economic stimulation with credit creation and government spending programs can only come about through the transfer of wealth from productive individuals.

While I was in Congress, the issue of paper money versus gold was rarely discussed on the House floor. A politician can afford to be complacent with a subject as complex as our banking system. And for this reason most members and their staffs ignore the subject and are not interested in discussing needed reforms.

This ignorance can be used to our advantage because, once enough citizens are informed, they can exert pressure on the majority of the members of Congress who have neither emotional nor self-serving interests in maintaining a powerful central bank. Once the banking system weakens further, and it's clearly in the interest of members' constituents to reform the system, our efforts to restore integrity to the monetary system will receive political support.

Since the Federal Reserve System is poorly understood, our educational efforts are equally as important as political action. It is, however, not too early to persistently point out to our representatives in Congress the evils of unlimited credit creation as it exists today, and why $200 billion annual deficits are not possible without such a system in place. Honest money must gain the moral highground and remove the corrupt political paper system. Although paper money is defended by high-minded people claiming prosperity for everyone, it leads instead to poverty and suffering for millions of innocent victims.

The inflation of the 1920s gave us the Great Depression of the 1930s; the monetary inflation of the late 1970s brought us the severe recession of 1980-1983; the inflation of 1982-1987 will give us the great depression of the late 1980s. The victims are those who lose their jobs and whose standards of living are continuously eroded with higher costs of living. The so-called benefits of economic stimulation with credit creation and government spending programs can only come about through the transfer of wealth from productive individuals. This transfer of wealth, regardless of how complicated the process is, is no more moral than if the beneficiaries took a gun and robbed their neighbors.

Honest money must come into circulation through honest work and effort and be a commodity, voluntarily used by all the participants in the transactions. No legal-tender laws are needed to compel its use if an honest monetary system is in place.

Reforms

Control over money conveys great power to those managing the system and is not going to be given up easily. The people have been taught to believe that inflation is to their benefit,even if they do not understand the mechanism by which it comes about.

Mises said in *The Theory of Money and Credit*: "Inflation is the true opium of the people administered to them by anti-capitalistic governments and parties."

Opium can kill, yet initially it makes one feel good. The same is true of inflation. The whole misconception about inflation comes from assuming that credit or currency creation is synonymous with wealth creation. Yet the opposite is true, for inflation destroys wealth, misdirects the economy, and brings on social strife. The early stimulation and apparent benefits brought about by new money are always at the expense of someone else. It robs rather than creates.

Samuel Johnson in the *Rambler* said that this attempt to create wealth without effort was, "the reigning error of mankind." Attaining wealth and a decent standard of living by mysticism, deceit, or fraud cannot work in the future and never has worked in the past. Instead, the results of inflation have always been anger, loss of trust in the government, economic and social turmoil, and frequently war.

It is not difficult to get the average person to understand, with a brief explanation, why excessive money and credit is unwise. The bigger problem is to get a consensus on how to stop the federal deficits and to end the process of credit creation by the Federal Reserve System. The political problem of cutting any portion of the budget is overwhelming. The transition to sound money is feared even by some of its advocates, due to the magnitude of the problems we face.

Instituting sound money is fraught with problems, but in comparison to the problems associated with runaway inflation, they are not nearly as dangerous. Fearing the pain of a lifesaving operation should never prompt one to reject it.

Is Monetarism a Solution?

The Monetarists claim the answer to our monetary problem is to increase the money supply at a slower rate; for example, between 3 percent and 5 percent a year. They correctly see the relationship between the money supply and the subsequent higher prices, the economic distortion, and the unemployment, yet they cling to the belief that a modest, steady monetary inflation will solve all the problems inherent in the unwise system of the past 50 years.

Monetarists fail to see that all prices do not go up symmetrically. With any inflation at all, economic distortion and malinvestment will take place.

Milton Friedman in *Free to Choose* claims money growth at ten percent a year, if steady, "would do no great harm," but disavows such a policy because it would then be too "tempting" for the money managers to inflate at a greater rate. Friedman adds:

> All of these adjustments are set in motion by changes in the rates of monetary growth and inflation. If monetary growth were high and steady, so that, let us say, prices tended to rise year after year by 10 percent, the economy could adjust to it. Everybody would come to anticipate a 10% inflation; wages would rise at 10 percent a year more than they otherwise would; interest rates would be 10 percentage points higher than otherwise—in order to compensate the lender for inflation; taxes would be adjusted for inflation and so on and so on.
>
> Such an inflation would do no great harm, but neither would it serve any function. It would simply introduce unnecessary complexities in arrangements. More important, in such a situation, if it is ever developed, would probably not be stable. If it were politically profitable and feasible to generate a 10 percent inflation, the temptation would be great when and if inflation ever settled there, to make the inflation 11 or 12 or 15 percent. Zero inflation is a politically feasible objective! A 10 percent inflation is not. That is the verdict

of experience.

Friedman claims that if money is increased at five percent a year and productivity is five percent a year, prices remain stable and there is "no inflation." It is true that average prices may remain stable, but it's not true that there is no inflation or malinvestment.

The Austrian economists' view—that all prices, interest, and wages do not go up evenly—is vitally important in understanding why even a four or five percent inflation in the money supply per year will still cause harmful and serious cumulative effects. When money is increased at five percent per year, someone or some group must benefit from this new money, so the political problems of favoritism exist, even if it's on a lower scale.

The value of money cannot be fictitious, it must be real, and not susceptible to manipulation by the politicians or bankers or even the monetarists

---

Since prices do not respond evenly across the board as the monetarists wish, the zero-percent price increase they desire is just wishful thinking. Some prices will go up, others may drop. Even if it were true, it is obvious that the same argument that Friedman uses for the probable abuse of a ten percent inflation rate, also applies to the lower rate.

His solution for inflation—increase the quantity of money less rapidly—is like telling an alcoholic to drink *only* one pint of scotch per day instead of the usual two. Friedman fails to accept the Austrian explanation of the subjective theory of value for price setting, and endorses the mathematical explanation of prices.

Nevertheless Friedman tells us in his own words why we must have a hard currency, where the citizen is in charge, not government: "Since time immemorial, sovereigns—whether kings, emperors or parliaments—have been tempted to resort to increasing the quantity of money to acquire resources to wage war, construct monuments, or for other purposes."

Friedman accepts the Keynesian notion that money should not have intrinsic value, saying: "Though the value of money rests on a fiction, money serves extraordinarily useful economic functions."

That is the problem; the value of money cannot be fictitious, it must be real, and not susceptible to manipulation by the politicians or bankers or even the Monetarists. Friedman claims that inflation only occurs "when the quantity of money rises appreciably, more rapidly than output," thus tying his definition of inflation to productivity and not limiting it to the money supply alone.

This is where he differs from the free-market Austrian economists. Although productivity—if kept at the same level as the rate of monetary inflation he personally advocates—would prevent generalized price inflation, it would not prevent malinvestment. Yet, he criticizes those who blame "low productivity" for inflation, while using "productivity" to hide monetarist mischief in the economy.

How is he to guarantee five percent economic growth if he is already locked into a five percent money growth? Five percent new money can go into bidding of prices just as easily as ten percent. The subjective decisions made by consumers and businessmen together will tell us how the new money will be spent—no chart can predict the future, it can only tell us what was done in the past under previous circumstances.

Hayek, in his "Denationalization of Money", is critical of the monetarist approach as being "no more than a useful rough approximation to a really adequate explanation," pointing out that:

> ...a stable price level and a high and stable level of employment do not require or permit the total quantity of money to be kept constant or to change at a constant rate...No authority can beforehand ascertain and only the market can discover 'the optimal quantity of money.'

As to Friedman's reassurance that a legally fixed rate of money growth will insure stability and confidence, Hayek disagrees and predicts this very feature of monetarism would be the source of panic:

> I can only say that I would not like to see what would happen if under such a provision it ever became known that the amount of cash in circulation was approaching the upper limits and therefore a need for increased liquidity could not be met.

Quoting Roger Bagehot, Hayek says, 'The near approach to the legal limits of reserves would be a sure incentive to panic.'

Mises states that any amount of inflation of the money supply—even one percent—will produce a boom and a subsequent bust, even though a one percent inflation causes a less severe recession. This, he claims, will occur regardless of whether or not prices rise, stay the same, or even drop, because of the distortion of interest rates and ensuing bad business decisions. The timing is unpredictable and the extent to which the money may go into one industry versus another is not predictable, making outcome unpredictable as well.

The question may arise as to why an increase in the money supply by three to five percent, as the monetarists advocate, is so much different from a three to five percent increase in the gold supply if we're on a gold standard. The most important difference is that under government management, history proves that three percent will soon be six percent and the six percent soon will be twelve percent. Under gold the three percent will be three percent, or two percent, or even less due to the effort required to mine gold and the incentives that are determined by the purchasing power of gold.

But for the sake of argument, let us assume the government controlled three percent money growth is achievable. Why is this less advantageous than a gold standard with a three percent growth in its supply? Let us even assume prices in general remain stable under both conditions. Under the conditions of government-induced money growth, the new money enters the market under the direction of the government, and banks and businesses are privileged to receive this new money first. Malinvestment will still occur and a correction will be necessary. When gold is produced by effort, this commodity, used as money, enters the markets by purchasing goods and services. Decisions are made for these purchases or investments through the market, not by non-market political decisions such as occur with government-created money.

Getting government out of the money management business completely is the only answer

---

Retaining dictatorial powers over the money supply as the monetarists advocate, even though the rest of the economy has been turned over to the market, will not suffice. It is bad economics and it won't stop the inflation. But worse yet it slashes into personal liberties to such a degree that the defense of absolute natural rights becomes impossible, if it is conceded that government shall maintain this dictatorial power with a central bank. It will always be abused by the powerful at the expense of the weak.

The banker, the industrialist, the politician, and the welfare recipient will forever pressure the money managers to bend a bit and rationalize a need for monetary growth, always slightly more than originally intended. We must have a check on money growth with the people being able to prevent the continuous abuse of the money. Getting government out of the money management business completely is the only answer.

The Supply-Sider's Gold Standard

The supply-siders, as led by Jack Kemp and Arthur Laffer, have advocated a type of gold standard, but in truth it is nothing more than a pseudo-gold standard. It is actually a gold price rule whereby the Federal Reserve adjusts monetary policy dependent on the gold price.

However, the supply-siders are much more vocal when the gold price is low or steady than when it is rising. When the gold price is low or steady they are always pressuring the Federal Reserve to expand credit much faster. The supply-siders do not understand the price system and, therefore, do not understand that inflation of the money supply may not have a significant effect on prices until a year or two later.

The supply-siders never attack the omniscient power of the Federal Reserve. As a matter of fact, they are the Fed's best friends. Their main criticism has always been that credit expansion has been much too slow and advocate more rapid expansion of the money supply.

Taking the position that it is politically dangerous to criticize the federal deficit, the supply-siders must bear the responsibility for the massive deficits of the Reagan Administration. These deficits have prompted rapid inflation of the money supply in order to accommodate the spending.

History will show that great harm has been done by the supply-siders who, with conservative rhetoric, have actually championed deficit financing and massive monetary inflation. They have done this under the guise of friendship toward the gold standard; instead this has been nothing more than a charade. The supply-siders have actually pushed for a more rapid expansion of the money supply than the Keynesian liberals or the monetarists.

Eventually, we will see the disastrous results of such a policy as it will be translated into higher interest rates, rapid price inflation, and certainly much higher prices for the monetary metals, gold and silver.

Reform of the monetary system is obviously crucial to our economic survival. However, it is desperately important that the supply-sider's pseudo-gold standard gets no consideration whatsoever and is recognized for its distortion of a very sound principal—the gold standard. If it is not recognized that the supply-sider's gold standard is a danger and will undermine true monetary reform, we will end up with a monetary system no better than what we have.

Today's problem clearly can be placed at the doorstep of those who advocate paper money. If we accept a pseudo-gold standard, to the supply-siders'liking, any problems which evolve will be laid at the doorstep of the gold standard rather than at the doorstep of the supply-siders who have advocated deficit financing, massive monetary inflation, and a gold standard that is unworkable.

The answer to the monetary dilemma is to have a non-fraudulent, 100 percent reserve, gold-coin standard. A gold standard would eliminate all speculation about the political motivations of the monetary authorities in governing the supply of money. The great virtue of the gold standard is that it removes discretionary power of the money supply from any one agency, thus ending the most fertile source of speculation. The gold standard puts the power of the monetary system into the hands of the people and takes it away from the politicians and the bankers, thus removing a potential vehicle for establishing a tyranny.

Gold cannot be mined as cheaply as Federal Reserve Notes can be printed, nor can its supply be manipulated on a daily basis. There is a great dispersion of power with a gold standard.

That is the strength of the system, for it allows the people to check any monetary excesses of their political leaders and does not allow the leaders to exploit the people by debasing the money.

A particular virtue of the gold standard deserves our attention. The monetarists concede that the supply of money is of the utmost importance in understanding inflation and that its control is crucial. Even the most dedicated Keynesians do not advocate uncontrolled increase of the money supply, recognizing the obvious consequences of overly rapid monetary expansion, yet failing to see the problem with modest rates of monetary growth. With commodity money, the advantage is that the money supply is independent of the politicians, government bureaucrats, and the banks. Mises states:

> This is its (the gold-standard's) advantage. It is a form of protection against spendthrift governments. If under the gold-standard, a government is asked to spend money for something new, the Minister of Finance can say: 'And where do I get the money? Tell me first how I will find the money for this additional expenditure.'

The temptation on the part of the politicians to avoid asking "where do we get the money?" is so powerful that virtually all resort to the easy way out—financing debt through money creation. The problem is less economic than political.

Most of those involved, although they are not likely to admit it, know that financing government debt with inflation of the money supply cannot go on forever and is a deception that will eventually become known to everyone. It is just that the politician figures it will be later and not sooner and he will not have to bear the responsibility of the economic problems he has caused.

The belief by most that the corrective action needed to stop inflation will cause pain and suffering prompts the delay in making the needed exchanges. It must be realized that if inflation is stopped swiftly and completely, suffering will be minimal. But this suffering must be blamed on the inflation, and not on those making the difficult decisions to stop the fraud. We must also remember that we are not likely to restore soundness to our money as long as the people retain an insatiable appetite for government welfare programs for both rich and poor.

Those hostile to commodity money refer derogatorily to going "back" on the gold-standard. We need not be pushed into defending an old monetary system. Although gold has been used literally for thousands of years as money, its refinement as modern money, either government-protected or free-market managed, has not been achieved. Its greatest success was reached in the nineteenth century and permitted the great economic growth of that time. Even then it was far from perfect and ultimately failed as government refused to abide by the rules, especially in times of war.

There is obviously a lot of room for modernization and sophistication of a gold standard. The best system has probably not even been thought of yet. Its modern features should be emphasized, not its antiquity. For instance, Hayek in advocating free-market money, is convinced that the market, not the government, can achieve the best monetary system, just as it solves all other problems in the most efficient manner. He even questions whether or not the metals would be chosen as the most convenient form of money.

My interpretation of monetary history is that if the choice were completely left to the market, gold would be chosen as the foundation of the monetary system. Of course, in leaving it to the market to decide, the exact outcome is not predictable. Only a better solution than that proposed by governments throughout the ages would be found.

We are not likely to restore soundness to our money as long as the people retain an insatiable appetite for government welfare programs for both rich and poor.

Free-market money—a very advanced idea of freedom—will not likely be achieved in the foreseeable future. But an improved government gold standard, better than any previously devised, certainly could be. It would not be difficult if prevailing attitudes were agreeable to develop a 100 percent redeemable gold coin standard, and this would certainly be an improvement on the fractional reserve standards used in the past and always abused.

The two most common concerns expressed regarding a gold standard are:

1. Is there enough gold in the world for us to go on a gold standard?

Yes, there is certainly enough gold in the world to maintain a gold standard. The exact amount of gold is of little importance as long as all prices are allowed to adjust freely. The purchasing power of gold must be allowed to vary on a free market. If goods and services expand more rapidly than the gold supply, prices will fall and relatively speaking the money supply expands. The gold supply historically has expanded at a two-to-three percent annual rate. The incentive to mine more gold will be related to its purchasing power. When prices are low in terms of gold, mining expands; when the supply of gold rises and prices rise there is less incentive to mine gold. The market process adjusts the supply of money through mining incentives and price changes.

The fear of not having enough gold to support the system is unfounded. The real fear should be the excessive money and credit created by the Federal Reserve. Under a gold standard, credit created freely in the market place is allowed to occur but it is measured in the gold unit of account and cannot be distorted by politicians or central bankers.

The often-repeated concern about a gold shortage under a gold standard is a reflection of Keynesian economic thought. For decades, American economic students have been taught that economic growth is totally dependent on stimulatory money growth, which is not true.

Real economic growth is dependent upon incentives to produce, the ability to control the wealth produced and a willingness to save on the part of the producers, the true source of capital. Capital and economic growth is not dependent upon an expanding money supply whether it be paper or gold. The answer to this concern is that any amount of gold will suffice as long as prices are allowed to adjust freely.

2. Won't a gold standard place too much power in the hands of the Soviet Union and South Africa, the key world producers of gold?

The concern that the gold standard would place too much power in the hands of South Africa and the Soviet Union is a "red" herring. At the rate the Soviet Union produces gold each year, it would take them one hundred years to double the world supply. Anyone who can control only one percent of the supply on an annual basis of a commodity has no practical control over its value.

In contrast, the Federal Reserve could double the money supply under today's circumstances any day of the year it desires. Even if the Soviet Union could affect the gold standard and do damage to our monetary system by either withholding or dumping gold onto the market, it would not serve their interest to do so. They certainly were not able to do so when the dollar was fixed at $35 to an ounce. They have benefited more since the gold standard has been abandoned in 1971, with gold fluctuating, than when it was fixed at $35. The ability to affect or destroy a gold market or a gold standard is no different than the Soviet's ability to fix the price of wheat with a controlled production. The only difference would be that it is much harder to manipulate the gold market because of the difficulty in producing large amounts of gold.

These two concerns are frequently expressed by those who detest the use of gold because it threatens the power they achieve with a paper money system. The truth is that we need not be concerned about the total supply of gold in the world nor should we worry about the Soviet Union threatening our monetary system if we restore the gold standard.

The answer—for those who challenge gold as archaic—is that inflation is archaic. Throughout history kings have debased the metals in order to inflate. Fraud associated with money is an ancient tradition. A non-fraudulent commodity money is one of the most modern freedom ideas known to man. It is the fear of change and a clinging to the past, that compels men to reject gold and endorse inflation.

Ultimately though, we will be compelled to make a change in the monetary system, whether we want to or not. Even then, the choice will be between another fraudulent system and a system demanding honesty, with the people in charge, and not the bankers or the government.

Some Positive Steps Toward Gold

Although our current economic and financial conditions are deteriorating, some positive monetary events have occurred over the past twelve years. The old Bretton-Woods, pseudo-gold standard breathed its last on August 15, 1971. Since then the U.S. economy has suffered from sharps swings of inflation and recession with a steady erosion of the average family's standard of living. Nevertheless it was not long after the collapse of the Bretton-Woods fixed exchange rate system that economic and political forces were put in motion, laying the foundation for an eventual return to gold.

Everyday, more and more Americans become aware of our fraudulent monetary system and seek refuge from it by owning hard assets

---

After forty years, the right of American citizens to own gold was once again restored in January 1975 (thanks to the work of Jim Blanchard and Congressman Phil Crane). In 1977 Senator Jesse Helms and his legislative assistant Howard Segemark were instrumental in legalizing gold clause contracts, a right taken from us by FDR and the liberal courts in the 1930's. Although these contracts are not yet commonly used, this legal step is of great importance to the hard money movement.

Today, as a consequence of the insidious government-caused inflation, there is a healthy and growing interest in gold, both as an investment and as money. The respect and understanding for gold is better now than it was in the 1930's when the American people complacently allowed FDR and his cronies to confiscate the people's gold.

During the Great Depression, the people passively gave up their right to own gold out of fear and lack of understanding about gold. Also the paper dollar at that time was rising in value due to deflation of the money supply. None of these conditions exist today. Instead there is more determination than ever for gold owners not to relinquish their gold even if it were called in.

Since we are seeing no deflation, and paper money is continuing to lose its value, there exists a lot more incentive to keep the gold out of the hands of an untrustworthy government. And today's distrust of governments is understandably quite high. Everyday, more and more Americans become aware of our fraudulent monetary system and seek refuge from it by owning hard assets. This growing multitude will help hold back the aggressive hand of government while providing the nucleus of sound thinking necessary to lead us to a trustworthy monetary system.

A Major Event after 53 Years

Shortly after FDR was sworn into office, the Emergency Banking Act of 1933 was passed. Gold was soon confiscated from the people and gold coins ceased to circulate. Those who continued to hold gold other than numismatic coins became criminals. Other than the unsuccessful gold arts medallion program of the 1970's, U.S. gold coins were not minted again until 1986.

The ultimate hedge against monetary debasement is gold. It is essential for the average person to be able to hold gold in easily recognizable coins of assured quality. This ultimate hedge—the gold coin—is also the foundation on which a sound money is built. Authentic gold coinage, with full legal rights for citizens to own and transport them at will, is essential in rebuilding and maintaining a sound system of money.

Although a remnant of economists and freedom fighters argued for gold ownership and a gold standard for decades after Roosevelt confiscated the gold, it was not until the 1970s that serious thought was given to it. But the clear failure of the Bretton-Woods Agreement in 1971 offered an opportunity to the gold advocates.

Monetary shambles encouraged them to work harder, and many anti-gold people convinced themselves that Federal Reserve Notes and Special Drawing Rights (SDRs) could serve as money, believing it was no longer necessary to oppose the pro-gold forces who were arguing for the right of gold ownership. Once gold ownership was made legal, many countries, especially South Africa, Canada, and Mexico, quickly started selling gold coins to the American people. This set the stage for the United States once again, after fifty-three years, to start minting legitimate gold coins.

My interest in monetary policy and the gold standard provided a strong incentive for me to enter politics. It was probably not a coincidence that my first congressional race occurred in 1974, the same year gold legalization was passed (ownership became legal January 1, 1975).

The tragic economic events associated with wage and price controls between 1971-1974 confirmed to me firsthand the assumptions made by the Austrian hard-money economists. The pro-gold, hard-money economists were the only ones who could explain the predicament in which we found ourselves. This prompted me to insist that I be placed on the Banking Committee once elected to Congress, so I could concentrate on promoting sound monetary policy.

Although a great deal of effort was exerted by my staff and me in pursuing this goal over the years, it wasn't until the fall of 1980 that a real breakthrough occurred. My amendment (Jesse Helms introduced the same amendment in the Senate) to the IMF bill to establish the Gold Commission was passed and signed into law by Jimmy Carter on October 7, 1980. Tip O'Neill, at the request of the Republican leadership, appointed me to one of the four House slots in the 17-member Commission.

For six months—from the fall of 1981 until the spring of 1982—the Commission met at the Treasury Building to fulfill the congressional mandate "to study the role of gold in the domestic and international monetary systems." The Commission's report to Congress was submitted March 31, 1982. The minority report was published as *The Case For Gold* (authored by Lew Lehrman and me).

I believe that when the monetary history of this period is written, the much larger majority report will have little bearing and that it will be said that *The Case For Gold* was helpful in restoring sound money. Already, many more people have read *The Case For Gold* than have waded through the massive and rambling majority report.

The seventeen-member Commission was biased toward paper money and internationalism. The Establishment was well-represented with three members of the Federal Reserve Board, the Secretary of the Treasury, two members of the President's Council of Economic Advisors, four

House Members, three Senators, and four private citizens. Of the seven Members of Congress, I was the only one favorable to gold; two of the private citizens were also favorable. From the beginning, it was a foregone conclusion that there would be no recommendation from the Commission supporting a gold standard.

But all Washington activities are political. Although the large majority of the Commission were hostile to gold, the philosophic groundwork of the past several decades had an influence on popular opinion which did influence the Gold Commission members' thinking. It was the existence of a gold movement that prompted the Gold Commission to consider and recommend the resumption of gold-coin mintage after five decades.

This Commission recommendation was crucial because Congress does pay attention to a commission it creates. The feeling of the majority was that a concession would pacify those wanting a gold standard and yet not be construed as condoning or encouraging a gold standard. Though the anti-gold people believed they were merely "throwing us a bone," it was a major victory in our efforts to restore sound money in the United States.

As soon as the Commission made its report to Congress, I introduced a bill to satisfy the Commission's recommendation. A gold coin bill did not pass until 1985, and only after several revisions. My original intent was to get Congress to mint a gold coin capable of circulating as money parallel to the Federal Reserve Notes. This meant a coin denominated by weight and not by dollars and without legal tender status. My bill would have exempted the coin from capital gains and sales tax and would have had it minted from existing U.S. gold stocks. Final passage of the bill came with minimal opposition, since the support for it included a coalition of leftists who saw it as a slap at South Africa and a way to hinder the massive sale of Krugerrands in the United States.

By the time the coin bill was passed, my original was modified a great deal. Ridiculous dollar amounts were placed on each of the four coins ($50 for the one ounce and $10 for the quarter ounce, for example). They were made legal tender for values with no monetary significance, but this satisfied the Fed and the Treasury, as well as a vocal group of coin collectors. The coin was not made exempt from capital gains taxes, thus making it impossible for it to truly compete with Federal Reserve Notes not similarly handicapped.

In spite of all the coins' shortcomings, however, the resumption of one of the few constitutionally authorized functions of Congress (the minting of gold coins) was truly a monumental event of historic significance. And along with the minting of the gold coins, a silver ounce coin was also authorized.

To ensure the survival of a sound monetary system, we can abolish the Federal Reserve and privatize its one useful function—check-clearing

---

Over the past fifteen years, the troy ounce has become the unit most associated with gold and silver coins. Nearly a dozen countries are now minting gold and silver ounce coins. The concept that money is a weight and not a piece of paper with zeros on it is crucial in our efforts to achieve sound money.

This step toward sound money was of great importance, but it is important that the momentum continues. The tragic economic conditions that paper money always bring will continue. Proper blame must be placed for our problems on our current monetary system.

We must also demand the establishment of a gold coin standard, the repeal of legal tender laws, an audit of the Fed, putting the Fed on budget, and elimination of power of the Fed to create credit (whether to stimulate the economy or monetize federal debt). To ensure the survival of a sound monetary system, we can abolish the Federal Reserve and privatize its one useful function—check-clearing.

Freedom and sound money go hand-in-hand. Freedom cannot survive without honest money. Honest money will never exist in a country with a non-market economy. Money cannot be isolated and thought of as separate from the concept of liberty.

A free society must incorporate a precise understanding of the nature of money. If we do not understand the close connection between liberty and money, we will help to perpetuate the greatest fraud in the history of man—today's worldwide debasement of the monetary system. Instituting a sound monetary system requires that we eliminate the oppressive hand of government in all areas of society.

No one should underestimate the potential calamity that we face if we do not address the subject of sound money and a free society.

SUMMARY

Have We Lost Respect?

The twentieth century has not been kind to the principles of freedom. The U.S. Constitution sadly has lost essentially all its meaning. This document was intended to keep the government small and the individual important, but today we find the opposite; the government is all-powerful and individual liberty is on the wane and poorly understood. The Constitution was intended to restrain the power of government's being nothing more than a document of "Thou Shalt Nots." The Founding Fathers intended to make the passage of laws and the imposition of taxes cumbersome and difficult, but today we find big government expands routinely with little restraint and no remorse.

The Anti-Federalists, who warned of the Constitution's weaknesses were right. The concept of the role of government has dramatically changed over the past 200 years. Instead of the government's being "we" and "us," it is now, "them" and "they". Most people assume the government is a source of material benefit and privilege, not an instrument to guarantee freedom for the individual. Instead of equal rights and equal justice, there now is merely competition in trying to avoid becoming a victim. The victimization is required to satisfy someone else's preconceived notion of economic equity, equal opportunity, and equal distribution of the loot confiscated by government.

Instead of limited government's guaranteeing our liberties, we have been given runaway government, runaway deficits, and runaway spending, with great importance placed on the politicians and the power they wield in Washington and state legislatures. The ability of lobbyists is of much greater importance to the economic success of an individual or corporation than their ingenuity and ambition.

Government is totally out of control in its expansive role in our personal and business lives. The concept of rights has been completely muddled. Deficits are no longer frowned upon and have literally become a way of life, not only for our government but for corporations and individuals as well. Fiat money has become an accepted institution and a tool of the wealthy elite and the political establishment.

We have been following a run-a-muck foreign policy—designed to police the world, yet this policy has made us vulnerable and weak and does nothing for peace and safety for Americans. Fear of nuclear war is no longer a concern of the few. Our foreign policy is based on self-sacrifice of the American taxpayer and unrealistic idealism. The special interests of the military-industrial complex, the banking elite, and socialist dictators have controlled policy for practically the entire twentieth century. America's interests have been ignored and the citizen's rights trampled on. Wars now are being fought without declaration and without any intent to win.

During this same period of time, we have also lost respect for the spiritual value of human life. As Samuel Adams warned us, "Our manners have become universally corrupt." We place relative value on life as we justify abortion and at the same time we place relative value on liberty, allowing our young innocent men to be drafted to fight no-win wars for the wealthy business and banking elite.

A truly free society, dedicated to maximum liberty for all, that ignores the important issue of all life, including fetal life, will have a difficult time defending its position on other matters. Failure to deal philosophically with the issue of a three-pound fetus inadvertently born alive during an abortion procedure and subsequently drowned by the abortionist will discredit the freedom movement.

A calloused attitude toward the unborn permits a calloused attitude toward the newborn, the elderly, and the deformed—as well as toward all principles of liberty.

We should be neither surprised nor shocked that we hear frequent stories of newborns being thrown in ditches to die. Vocal support for infanticide and euthanasia is now common. We live in an age where child abuse is of epidemic proportions. Our emergency rooms are flooded with battered children, and the social philosophers search for the cause.

Some who talk of children's rights fail to see the importance of life itself. In their search for perfect liberty, they mistakenly claim children have a right not to be subject to parental controls. Until it is recognized that all life is of the utmost importance, solving the problems of child abuse and defining children's rights will be impossible.

Without this the erosion of liberty will continue. A careless attitude toward the sanctity of life can hardly prompt an energetic and intellectually acceptable defense of individual rights. No one I know, including those who accept abortion as an absolute right of the mother, relishes the horror of dismemberment of a small, but quite viable human life.

The Roe vs. Wade decision legalized abortion up until the day prior to birth. In the United States there are 120,000 late abortions (after-three-month gestations) each year, even though there are 7500 serious complications annually from this procedure. Since 1973 the maternal mortality rate for abortions after the fourth month has been higher than for childbirth.

Society's attitude toward liberty is totally dependent on society's respect for all life. This problem is more an ethical one than legal. No legislation or constitutional amendment can instill this very-much-needed respect for life. Samuel Adams was right that no law or constitution can solve our problems if "the manners of a society are universally corrupt." A hardened attitude condoning and encouraging abortion will do great harm in undermining all our efforts to guarantee one's absolute right to one's own life.

We who promote libertarian ideas are proud of our high moral standard regarding nonaggression. These same standards must apply to all life as well as to all liberty.

Even if we resent the use of government to resolve this dilemma, it is nevertheless imperative that our respect for all human life—small as well as large—whether in the womb or in the crib—is clearly expressed. A society that does not recognize the special value of all human life cannot survive. Compassion for the truly unfortunate, the weak, the infirm, and those who cannot defend themselves because of size or age is a characteristic of a civilized society.

If life has no spiritual value, what makes liberty worth preserving? If life itself is not very special, how can working for liberty be justified?

Historic Contest

The ongoing crisis to preserve liberty is truly an historic struggle of great proportion and is destined to worsen. The contest is clearly between those who advocate individual liberty and those who indiscriminately use government power for their own benefit. Although this battle between liberty and government force is ages old, it is once again currently of vital importance.

The competitive forces clearly show that there is an ongoing struggle between those acting in self-interest with responsibility and those who, through government action, would control others for reasons of personal gain, personal ego, or misdirected benevolence. It is a contest between self-reliance and that of dependency, security, and the use of other men's productive efforts—a battle that literally is as old as recorded history.

The convictions of our Founding Fathers were strong enough for them to take on the British, while today the abuse of power by our own government, although far worse than that of the King, prompts little action.

History has given us periods of stability with both relative freedom and relative slavery. When conditions exist where there is more slavery than freedom, we have experienced stagnation. When there has been relative freedom, as certainly there has been during the existence of the United States, there has been moderate growth and prosperity.

Although agitation and discontent can smolder for long periods, eventually the contest between those who are enslaved and those who would enslave others explodes as does a dormant volcano. The conditions for violent revolution vary from generation to generation. Many ingredients other than the length of time of calmness determine when events lead to more violent and radical changes. They include prevailing ideas, determination of the leaders, the nature of the enemy, the ruthlessness of those in power, the ability to mobilize large numbers of people, and the emotional appeal of the leaders.

The convictions of our Founding Fathers were strong enough for them to take on the British, while today the abuse of power by our own government, although far worse than that of the King, prompts little action. The patriotic citizens of colonial days brought about a major revolution with a positive change in favor of individual freedom—a unique episode of man's history and something that ought to be duplicated again.

Today's oppression is entrenched and a great threat, but is nevertheless tolerated by most Americans. The numbers of those who are resentful of government's abuse are growing, and this is a positive sign. The country's wealth is being consumed, and when it is clear that we are once again a poor nation, general resentment will emerge among the people. A recent study has predicted a million homeless by the year 2000. Failure to regain respect and understanding for individual rights will lead to violence.

Although the kettle of agitation is simmering, it is not yet boiling. The fires of discontent are not going to be turned off but are destined to be fueled by compounding political and economic errors. Freedom itself is at stake.

In spite of the crisis, there are great opportunities for the friends of freedom to change things for the better. There are great dangers if we are not organized; there is a great risk if plans are not laid. We cannot succeed without a philosophic commitment to freedom and we cannot organize without dynamic leadership. People must have hope, and this hope must outweigh the feeling of desperation. It must be understood that the need for revolutionary change need not be violent.

Tenacity of Power

Today's simmering economic, social, and political problems will eventually boil over. The contest will eventually be clear to everyone. Big-government advocates will spare no abuse, no resources, no cost, no tricks, no force in order to maintain the status quo of state power.

Statism itself will be at stake and those in power will feel threatened. They will easily win unless the determination of we who love freedom is superior to the desires of those in charge to cling to their power.

Everyone has a role to play. The segment of society that is philosophically committed to big government will be tenacious in their endeavors as they see themselves in a death struggle.

The many who are complacent about conditions around them will be the largest group and will be the bellwether of the apparent success of the two major factions. Some of these will go with the winners, some will go with the most vocal leaders, and some will go with the group they think will best provide for what they see is in their best interest in the nature of security. Complete complacency is an act in itself in that it is the absence of action that will permit one or the other faction to win. The masses are important, but never lead, and they need only to be convinced and guided.

Friends of freedom must quickly assemble and plan strategy. Everyone has a vital interest in the outcome. Broad agreements are crucial; arguing minute details of solutions to difficult problems can undermine the movement and become purely negative. Perfection by man in the struggle for freedom is not achievable. Denial of personality differences and legitimate differences of opinion are a mistake. Refusing to agree on generalized and precise principles guarantees failure.

It is possible for some who claim kinship to the freedom movement to inadvertently serve the statists by undermining the important work on which we can agree. Agreeing on the libertarian principal of nonaggression is worthwhile. Demanding that everyone agree on every single cent in the defense budget is nonproductive. Human beings are imperfect, and no one person or collective wisdom of any body or body of persons can produce perfect solutions. Intellectual collectivism should not replace a single person's individuality to think for himself and defend freedom while agreeing on broad principles.

Once one is committed and has chosen a side, the obligation to act is clear. Efforts must be educational, political, organizational, and financial. Each of us can use one or all of these tools to promote the cause of freedom.

Clearly the fundamental flaw of the twentieth century has been our loss of love for freedom and self-reliance while accepting the use of government to promote special interest in the name of individual rights. This low regard for the principles of freedom has prompted the political economic crisis in which we find ourselves. A precise plan is crucial to our survival and mandates that all of us join in this historic opportunity to restate the principles of freedom.

Vision of a Free Society

A truly free society is one that offers the greatest hope for peace and prosperity. The moral defense of the individual's right to life and liberty associated with the prosperity that can only come from a free market makes it easy to defend. However, the marketing of this ideal has not been successful.

A totally free market, operating with a sound currency, should delight everyone. The thought of no record-keeping for the government, paying no personal or corporate income taxes, should thrill every citizen.

Yet this is what was intended by the Founding Fathers. It's only a twentieth-century phenomenon to be involved in keeping and making available to the government unbelievable amounts of financial information—and then having it used against us without due process of law.

Sound money, no Federal Reserve, no business cycle, no inflation, low interest rates, high savings rates, trust in the future value of the money, capital accumulation! What a delight it would be to have an end to the confiscation of wealth through monetary debasement and once again see the reindustrialization of the United States. Instead of the government's being the counterfeiter, it would enforce the laws against counterfeiting of paper money.

In a free and prosperous society, labor shortages would be the problem, not unemployment. Instead of aliens being resented, they would be welcomed to serve our needs as our standard of living increases. What a delight it would be to see the reversal of our declining standard of living, which has been occurring over the past sixteen years. This can only come about by freeing the marketplace and introducing sound money.

A free society guarantees freedom of movement and, above all, absolute privacy. Moving our wealth in and out of the country would be of no concern to the government. Complete privacy guarantees individual liberty. Our personal lifestyles, as well as our religious lifestyles would be our business and ours alone. Instead of the government's forcing contracts on us and breaking those they make with us, the government would help enforce the contracts to which we voluntarily agree.

A free society offers the greatest chance for world peace. Free movement of people, goods, and ideas across borders makes a lot more sense than the uncontrolled sale and transfer of weapons across borders. A policy of neutrality and friendship to all makes a lot more sense than subsidies to our sworn enemies and our rich allies. Financing both sides of all the battles around the world, as we have been doing for the past forty years, must come to an end.

Free markets, sound money, balanced budgets, no income tax, civil liberties, and nonintervention in the internal affairs of other nations is the road to peace and prosperity.

How can the American people reject it?

About the Author

Ron Paul was elected four times to the United States Congress from Houston, Texas, as a Republican. As a Member of the Banking Committee, he worked to establish a gold standard and curb the Federal Reserve. He was also the House sponsor of the U.S. Gold Commission and co-author of its minority report: *The Case for Gold*.

A nationally known speaker and writer, he is also founder of the Council for Monetary Reform, chairman of the FREE Foundation; chairman of the Committee to Abolish the Fed, editor and publisher of *The Ron Paul Investment Letter*, distinguished counsellor to the Ludwig von Mises Institute, and a physician.

For his uncompromising advocacy of liberty, Congressman Paul won awards from the National Taxpayers Union (for the most pro-taxpayer record *ever*), the Council for a Competitive Economy, the Mises Institute, and the American Economic Council.

Ron Paul was born in Pittsburgh, Pennsylvania, in 1935. He received his BA from Gettysburg College and his MD from Duke University Medical School and was a flight surgeon in the U.S. Air Force. Dr. Paul and his wife Carol are the parents of five children and the grandparents of four. They make their home in Lake Jackson, Texas.

Other books by Ron Paul

The Case for Gold
Gold, Peace, and Prosperity
Ten Myths About Paper Money
Abortion and Liberty
Farewell Address to Congress
Mises and Austrian Economics—a Personal View

The Ludwig von Mises Institute

The Ludwig von Mises Institute, founded in 1982, is the research and educational center of classical liberalism, libertarian political theory, and the Austrian School of economics. Working in the intellectual tradition of Ludwig von Mises (1881-1973) and Murray N. Rothbard (1926-1995), with a vast array of publications, programs, and fellowships, the Mises Institute, with offices in Auburn, Alabama, seeks a radical shift in the intellectual climate as the foundation for a renewal of the free and prosperous commonwealth. This student series is one division of a larger publishing program that offers new and classic works in high-quality editions. For more information and ordering, see mises.org

Ludwig von Mises Institute
518 West Magnolia Avenue
Auburn, Alabama 36832-4528
334.321.2100 · Phone
334.321.2119 · Fax
contact@mises.org